THE
MAKING
OF A
DRUG-FREE
AMERICA

PROGRAMS THAT WORK

Mathea Falco

Foreword by Michael Crichton, M.D.

Times Books

Library of Congress Cataloging-in-Publication Data

Falco, Mathea.
    The making of a drug-free America : programs that work / Mathea Falco.
        p.   cm.
    ISBN 0-8129-6355-5
    1. Drug abuse—United States.   2. Narcotic addicts—Rehabilitation—United States.   3. Narcotics, Control of—United States.
I. Title.
HV5825.F335   1992
362.29′18′0973—dc20   92–53667

Book design by M. Kristen Bearse

Manufactured in the United States of America
9 8 7 6 5 4 3 2
First Paperback Edition

This book is dedicated to my son, Benjamin Falco Tarnoff,
and to all God's children.

AUTHOR'S NOTE

During the research for this book, I talked to hundreds of people across the country. To convey their views most directly, I have relied on quotes whenever possible. Some people preferred to remain anonymous, but wanted their voices heard. For these sources, I created fictitious first names and last initials and disguised their identities in other ways. I used full names only with the permission of the person quoted. In general, locations and program names are accurate. However, in Chapter 4, "Woodacres High School" is fictitious, although it is based on a real high school in Westchester County, New York.

I tried to avoid weighing down the narrative with academic references and reserved discussion of sources for chapter notes. Unless otherwise noted, statistics on drug use came from two major national annual surveys: the *National Household Survey on Drug Abuse* and *Drug Use Among American High School*

Seniors, College Students, and Young Adults. Specific quotes are taken from personal interviews or published documents.

I did not attempt to provide a comprehensive review of all drug programs nationwide. Rather, I described in detail some of the most promising ones, based on what we now know about prevention, education, treatment, and law enforcement. Space constraints forced me to be selective, and I hope that those who are not mentioned will understand.

ACKNOWLEDGMENTS

This project began in November 1988 when David Hamburg, the president of the Carnegie Corporation of New York, suggested to me that most Americans are pessimistic about drug abuse because they do not realize how much we already know about reducing the demand for drugs. He urged me to write a book that would explain recent research and describe programs which show real promise. Without his inspiration and encouragement, I would never have begun, and the generous support of the Carnegie Corporation made my work possible. I am grateful to Vivien Stewart and Elena Nightingale, also of Carnegie, for their many useful suggestions and sustaining interest.

To help set the direction for my work, David Hamburg convened a Substance Abuse Advisory Committee of public health, education, treatment, and prevention experts. The committee members were:

Gilbert J. Botvin, director, Institute for Prevention
Research, Cornell University Medical Center;
Lawrence S. Brown, professor, School of Public Health,
Columbia University;
James Burke, chairman, Strategic Planning Committee,
Johnson & Johnson;
Vanella Crawford, director, Project SPIRIT;
Sanford Dornbusch, director, Stanford Family Studies
Center;
Joy Dryfoos, author and researcher;
Robert Johnson, New Jersey College of Medicine and
Dentistry;
Lloyd Johnston, Institute for Social Research, University of
Michigan;
Stephen Joseph, former commissioner of health of the City
of New York;
David Lewis, director, Center for Alcohol and Addiction
Studies, Brown University;
Robert Karl Manoff, director, Center for War, Peace, and
the News Media, New York University;
Robert Millman, director, Drug and Alcohol Abuse
Services, Cornell University Medical Center;
Peter Reuter, director, Drug Policy Research Center, The
Rand Corporation;
Thomas Schelling, economist, University of Maryland;
S. Kenneth Schonberg, director, Division of Adolescent
Medicine, Montefiore Medical Center;
Kenneth Tewel, Queens College, City University of New
York;
Marta Tienda, Population Research Center, University of
Chicago.

The committee members and many others tirelessly an-
swered my questions, and the book reflects their wisdom. I

am especially grateful to Douglas Anglin, Naya Arbiter, James Burke, Joy Dryfoos, Lloyd Johnston, Mark Kleiman, Karol Kumpfer, Ellen Morehouse, Mary Ann Pentz, Susan Powers, Peter Reuter, Ken Warner, and Eileen Wasow. Three of my best teachers were my colleagues at the Cornell University Medical Center, Gilbert J. Botvin, Linda Dusenbury, and Robert Millman. They have all shaped my thinking but should not be held responsible for the final product.

Many people, most of whom must go unnamed, have contributed to this book by sharing their own experiences with drug abuse. They helped me understand the painful journey from addiction to recovery and the exhilaration of discovering the joys of living without drugs. Their insights moved me deeply.

I was immensely fortunate to have two imaginative, talented editors at Times Books. Peter Osnos skillfully guided the book from beginning to end, and Paul Golob cheerfully edited numerous drafts. Caroline Polk helped me update the book for paperback publication. Michael Crichton generously reviewed the manuscript and taught me much about clarity.

My husband, Peter Tarnoff, and my mother, Kathleen Fream Falco, provided inexhaustible support and good humor. My then six-year-old son, Benjamin, cheered me on during long hours of writing. Their love and laughter illuminate my life.

CONTENTS

FOREWORD

by Michael Crichton, M.D.

America's problems with drugs affect us all: when we ride a bus, a train, or a plane; when we send our children to school; when we walk home at night—or don't dare to. Drugs have become deeply interwoven in the everyday fabric of American life. And they are inescapable, found in every geographical region, every socioeconomic segment in our society. Drugs are truly a modern American plague. Our nation's policies toward drugs has been of concern to me since the days of my medical training, when I had a chance to observe at first hand both the human toll of illicit drug use and the inadequacy of our institutional responses to drugs in this country.

Not that we haven't taken action: the American government, recognizing the seriousness of our drug problem, has for nearly two decades waged a "war on drugs" to prevent them from entering the country. Since 1981 American taxpayers have spent more than $100 billion on reducing drug supplies. Unfortunately, by every measure, our attempts at interdiction have failed. Drugs on the street cost less today than they did a decade ago. Heroin costs only one-fourth what it did in 1981. Such inexpensive, readily available drugs has meant illegal drug use and its consequences continue to grow unchecked. Violent crime, much of it drug related, has increased 20 percent since 1988. Every two minutes, another drug-exposed baby is born. According to polls, 70 percent of Americans believe that the drug problem has grown worse in the last five years, and they are right.

The United States now has the highest rate of illegal drug use among all the nations of the industrialized world. Twenty-three million Americans over the age of twelve acknowledged using drugs last year—nearly one in ten. Six million Americans are addicts. A third of a million babies are born to addicted mothers every year. Drug and alcohol abuse are implicated in half of all violent crimes, and half of all automobile fatalities. In 1991 the Office of Management and Budget estimated the financial cost of drug and alcohol addiction—in lost productivity, illness, accidents, crime, and increased health-care costs— at an astonishing $300 billion per year. This is a sum greater than the amount we spend on national defense or on Social Security. It is greater than the interest on the national debt. But the enormous cost of America's drug problem is measured not merely in dollars but also in lives: some 40,000 Americans die of direct and indirect effects of drug use each year.

It is now undeniable that our long-standing policy to limit the supply of drugs in America has failed. But this is not because that effort has been carried out inadequately or ineptly. Quite the reverse: our war on drugs has been a well-funded, well-executed, bipartisan, long-term policy spanning six separate administrations, four Republican and two Democratic. Why, then, has it failed?

Few individuals are better qualified to answer this question than Mathea Falco, an international drug expert who has been closely involved with every aspect of U.S. drug policy for more than two decades. In the early 1970s, Ms. Falco was chief counsel to the Senate Judiciary Subcommittee on Juvenile Delinquency, directing hearings on delinquency and drug laws; then she was special assistant to the president of the Drug Abuse Council; and later she traveled around the world as assistant secretary of state for international narcotics matters. Leaving Washington in 1981, she spent several years as director of health policy at New York Hospital–Cornell Medical Center; during this time she traveled around the United States, assessing treatment and prevention programs and advising foundations on drug-related issues. Now she heads Drug Strategies, a Washington think tank focused on identifying effective approaches to combating substance abuse. To this new position she brings her consummate grace, high intelligence, and dedicated determination to help this country formulate an effective drug policy.

In *The Making of a Drug-Free America*, Falco addresses our earlier question: why has the "war on drugs" failed? Her answer is that policies based on interdiction are doomed from the outset. Halting the supply of drugs is not simply a matter of burning a few hundred acres in Colombia or in the Golden Triangle of Southeast Asia. Drugs are now a global business, produced in countries all around the world. In some nations, such as Burma, drug production is sanctioned by the government as a source of foreign currency. And our borders make us vulnerable; they are thousands of miles long, on both land and sea, and it has proved impossible to seal them against drugs. Most estimates suggest that interdiction has stopped less than 1 percent of the drugs coming into America. Finally, the technology of drug manufacture has shifted in recent years, so that more production now occurs at the street level. Drug dealers need less material from abroad than ever before. Given all these realities—global manufacturing, porous borders, and dealer-level production—America cannot realistically expect to keep drugs off our nation's street corners.

What, then, should we do? Falco argues that we must turn our national policy around, direct our attention homeward, and take steps to educate our citizens. If drugs have become woven into the fabric of American life, we must unweave them. Painstakingly, we must begin to remove drugs from our schools, our streets, and our workplaces. America, says Falco, will solve its drug problem only by reducing demand.

This is a much harder job than interdiction, and it calls for a fundamentally different approach. No longer can we wage war against villainous external enemies; instead, we must deal firmly and sympathetically with our fellow citizens, our children, and friends and neighbors. To this end, Falco proposes a balanced approach that includes drug-prevention programs in schools, treatment programs for citizens and prison inmates, and increased law enforcement to clean up our streets.

For years, Washington insiders have resisted change in drug policy on the grounds that it would be politically unacceptable. And yet the great majority of Americans agree with Falco that it is time for a change. Recent polls suggest that Americans have little faith in our drug policies: only 5 percent think elected officials are doing all they can, whereas 56 percent believe that elected officials are not really trying to solve the drug problem but merely give lip service to it. Only 11 percent of Americans expect our drug problem to get better in the next five years. More than half think it will get worse.

Asked how they would solve the drug problem, ordinary Americans are clear. They want a balanced approach. Nearly half would divide funds equally between law enforcement and programs for prevention, education, and treatment. Although

Americans favor stricter penalties for drug traffickers, they also recognize the importance of job opportunities and drug-treatment programs.

The emergence of this pragmatic, humane, comprehensive consensus reflects a growing personal experience with drug abuse in Americans' daily lives. Forty-five percent of those polled now say they personally know someone addicted to a drug other than alcohol. Often it is a close friend or family member. Forty percent say that drugs have forced them to change how they live, by making their homes more secure, avoiding certain places, or staying inside at night.

Americans understand that there are no easy answers to the modern plague of drugs. But they are convinced that it is not enough to burn crops in faraway countries or to patrol our borders with high-tech gadgetry. We've tried that—tried it for years—and it hasn't worked. Meanwhile the problem of drugs has come home, and Americans know it must be dealt with at home.

Let us hope that it does not take the politicians and the pundits too long to abandon their failed ideology and their failed programs, to catch up to the good common sense of the American people, and to finally institute an American drug policy that works.

The time is now. The need is pressing. This book by Mathea Falco points the way.

Santa Monica, California
April 1994

INTRODUCTION

TO THE

PAPERBACK EDITION

After two decades of combating drugs on the high seas and in the poppy fields of Asia, Americans have come to realize that it is time to bring the drug war home. In February 1994, a nationwide survey conducted by Peter Hart Research Associates found that Americans—by a margin of more than three to one—believe that we should be investing more resources in community drug education, treatment, prevention, and law enforcement programs rather than in efforts to cut off drug supplies coming into the country. At the same time, the American public is pessimistic: seven in ten consider drug abuse worse now compared to five years ago. And more than half think elected officials don't care about solving the drug problem.

Federal spending priorities are only now beginning to catch up with public opinion. In the 1992 presidential campaign, Bill Clinton pledged to make treatment on demand a reality and to provide effective prevention teaching in every school in America. But it was not until the spring of 1994 that he began to redeem those promises by proposing substantial funding increases for drug education and treatment in the 1995 budget. Even so, proposals such as this tend to wither on Capitol Hill, because skepticism persists over the effectiveness of demand reduction, especially as politicians perceive a need to appear "tough" on crime.

The push for more punitive solutions for drug-related crimes drives much of the current political debate. Yet this impulse to use prison as the primary response to drug crime will have costly consequences for years to come. To get candidates and voters to focus on those consequences, we must first publicize the harsh realities of our existing policies. Nationwide, we are spending $25 billion to imprison 1.35 million people—$18,500 per person per year. Two-thirds of these offenders have serious drug habits. Without intensive treatment, the cycle of addiction and crime will continue unabated after they leave prison. Yet fewer than 10 percent of these offenders currently get any drug treatment at all, even though treatment has been shown to cut recidivism by half.

In California, taxpayers are now spending more for prisons than for higher education. Under the new "three strikes and you're out" legislation, the state corrections budget will almost double by the end of the decade, jumping from $2.8 billion to $4.8 billion a year. Are these really the choices that Californians want to make? And what about the rest of America?

The 1994 Hart poll found that Americans actually prefer a balanced approach to the problem of drug abuse. While the public strongly believes (77 percent) that mandatory prison sentences for drug dealers will have a major impact in fighting drug crime, a large majority (64 percent) also think that job opportunities and training for drug offenders will make an important difference. Nearly half the public would divide antidrug spending equally between law enforcement and prevention, education, and treatment, while one-third would put more funds into prevention, education, and treatment. Only one in five Americans would put more money into drug law enforcement.

While many politicians continue to talk about drugs in loaded terms—describing programs as being "soft" or "hard" or "conservative" or "liberal"—the public has become essentially pragmatic. Above all, Americans want programs that work. We understand from our own experience in our homes, our schools, and our communities that the drug problem requires a wide range of solutions and that lasting success is possible only if we can reduce demand. A debate about more effective alternatives must be at the heart of all our discussions about crime and drugs. How can we be smart and tough, and create responsible policies that will not mortgage our future?

Communities across the country are finding their own answers to this question, built on programs that are having a significant impact on the drug problem. This book describes many of the most promising efforts, ranging from preschool prevention to antidrug media campaigns to intensive drug treatment in prison. In many places, the results are good. School programs that teach social skills and resistance training, like Life Skills Training and STAR, can reduce new drug use by half and new alcohol use by a third. Drug courts, which provide comprehensive treatment, supervision, and job training for first-time drug offenders, reduce addiction and crime for a fraction of the cost of incarceration. Long-term studies of prison programs have found that one year of intensive treatment before an offender is released can reduce recidivism by one-third to one-half. These programs pay for themselves the day the offenders walk out the prison gates because of the reduction in crime.

Although boot camps did not appear promising when I was conducting the initial research for this book, a new model in New York now shows positive results. The six-month program combines substance abuse treatment with rigorous discipline, academic education, and group counseling, all within a military-type structure. The program supports its graduates after release with employment, vocational training, peer-group counseling, and relapse prevention. Only 11 percent of the program graduates were returned to prison in the year following release, compared to one-third of those who had dropped out of boot camp and served their court-determined prison sentences. New York's Department of Correctional Services estimates that the first group of 6,400 boot camp graduates saved state taxpayers more than $200 million in prison construction and operating costs.

When I described the Miami drug court in the hardcover edition of this book, very little had been written about this new approach to nonviolent drug offenders. Since then, the drug court has proved cost-effective in reducing drug crime while still protecting the community. What began as an experiment in 1989 has become a widely accepted alternative to incarceration, supported by prosecutors, judges, and law enforcement officials. Drug courts now operate in two dozen cities, and the number continues to grow. The 1994 Violent Crime Control Act, which authorizes $28 billion to build new prisons, also provides $1.2 billion to expand drug courts.

The drug court's rapid journey from experimental model to national program shows the scope of public receptivity to treatment, particularly for criminal offenders. The program's popularity is due at least in part to its cost savings: Dade County taxpayers pay $16,000 to jail an inmate for a year compared to a price tag of about $1,000 for drug court. But the public has also come to recognize that treatment offers the best hope of breaking the deadly cycle of crime and addiction. The 1994 Hart poll found that a clear majority of Americans (59 percent) believe that rigorous, closely supervised treatment for first-time drug offenders makes a major difference in combating drug crime.

Despite growing public confidence in treatment for drug offenders, some people remain skeptical about the need for "treatment on demand." They argue that treatment does not work, since addicts often relapse and may require multiple treatment efforts. Research studies that have followed tens of thousands of addicts in treatment have found that relapse is part of the process of recovery. The single most important key to success is length of time in treatment. One-third of those who stay in treatment longer than three months are still off drugs a year later. When treatment lasts a year or longer, the success rate jumps to two-thirds.

Loose definitions of what constitutes treatment contribute to public confusion about effectiveness. The label "treatment" is used for a wide range of programs, from drop-in centers to highly structured residential communities to occasional drug education classes in prison. Not all approaches are equally effective. Several decades of research have found that successful programs have certain common characteristics: they are at least three months in duration; they are intensive, comprehensive, and highly structured; they require therapy focusing on all aspects of the addict's life; they include continuing participation in support groups; they provide access to educational, vocational, and employment opportunities; and they foster a sense of belonging to a community.

Although these programs work, they are still in short supply. Less than a third of the nation's 5.5 million addicts can get treatment unless they can afford to pay for private care. Even with President Clinton's proposed funding increase for 1995, treatment represents only 20 percent of the federal drug budget. State and local governments spend four times as much for drug enforcement as for treatment and prevention. A 1994 Rand Corporation study found that treatment is far more cost-effective in reducing illegal drug use than enforcement or interdiction. According to the study, providing treatment for all addicts would save more than $150 billion in social costs over the next fifteen years.[1]

Nearly one in two Americans have been personally touched by the drug problem: 45 percent of those surveyed in the 1994 Hart poll said that they know someone who became addicted to a drug other than alcohol. This personal knowledge sharply changes attitudes about how to deal with the problem: seven in ten believe that their addicted acquaintance would have been helped more by entering a supervised treatment program than by being sent to prison.

As the Hart poll confirms, the drug problem pervades our society, cutting across all social and economic groups. According to the 1992 National Household Survey, two-thirds of all current illegal drug users (those who used drugs in the month prior to the survey) are employed and three-quarters are white. Although drug use overall has declined by half since 1985, frequent cocaine use has remained unchanged. In the spring of 1994, drug overdose cases were up 9 percent over the previous year; heroin accounted for almost half these emergencies.

Among young people, drug use has gotten worse, not better, in the past two years. For the first time in a decade, junior high and high school students report substantially greater use of marijuana, LSD, stimulants, and cigarettes. Inhalants—like paint thinner, aerosol sprays, and airplane glue—have become an epidemic among children. Last year, one in five eighth graders reported sniffing inhalants, which produce instant highs but can be lethal. More ominously, teenagers now consider drugs and alcohol less harmful than they did four years ago, and they are more tolerant of drug use. Adults have similar attitudes: a majority see little harm in occasional drug use. These trends should sound alarms in every household in America: our children are threatened, and we have not yet made prevention our top priority.

In the past decade, we have learned that any lasting answer to the nation's drug problems must come from our communities. Government leadership is important, particularly in shaping public attitudes, and public funding is necessary to make comprehensive programs possible. But it is in our families, our schools, our churches, and our places of work that we come to understand what drug abuse means in personal terms. As many community coalitions have discovered, once the problem takes on a human face, people are quickly able to develop new strategies and to draw on new resources. And it is to give the drug problem a human face and to explore solutions that are already benefiting millions of Americans that I wrote this book.

Washington, D.C.
April 1994

THE
MAKING
OF A
DRUG-FREE
AMERICA

1

The
Supply-Side Seduction

The United States has the highest rate of drug abuse of any industrialized country in the world. Twenty-three million Americans used illicit drugs in 1992, almost half of them at least once a month. The vast majority of drug abusers are also heavy consumers of alcohol and tobacco.[1] The National Academy of Sciences estimates that 5.5 million Americans have serious drug problems that require treatment.[2]

Drug abuse is at the heart of what many people think has gone wrong with America. It appears as either the cause or the effect of a wide range of problems which seem out of control: urban blight, the destruction of families, the failure of schools, the loss of economic productivity. Drug abuse is also harder to ignore than most social problems. A Hart poll in 1994 reported that 45 percent of all Americans had had personal experience with drug abuse and drug dealing themselves or in their family or community.[3]

3

In recent years, Americans have come to consider drug abuse as a major threat to the nation's well-being, ranking with economic recession and environmental destruction. We worry about how to protect our children from addiction; we fear drug-related violence; we feel drugs are corroding our competitiveness in an increasingly difficult world.

Daily news reports feed our concerns. The horrors of drug abuse have become depressingly familiar: crack-addicted mothers abandoning their babies; young children dealing drugs instead of going to school; innocent citizens killed in gang shoot-outs; and sports stars dying from overdoses. Everyone wants to know what can be done.

■

The emergence of crack cocaine in the mid-1980s created a sense of national crisis. Cheap and rapidly addictive, crack—named for the cracking sound it makes when smoked—produces an extraordinarily intense euphoria that lasts ten to fifteen minutes. The sharp letdown that follows leaves users depressed and anxious. Driven to recapture the high, they become trapped in a cycle of compulsive use. Unlike heroin or marijuana, crack makes users aggressive, violent, and paranoid.[4] The consequences are often tragic. As one young mother who had sold her baby for more crack explained, "This drug will make you do anything. There's nowhere it won't make you go."

Crack quickly spread across the country, overwhelming America's law enforcement, drug treatment, and social service programs. Especially popular among women who dislike the disfiguring "track marks" which come from injecting drugs, crack further weakened many fragile single-parent families. Children became crack's indirect victims. Foster-care placements jumped by nearly a third from 1987 to 1990, mostly in

4

communities hard hit by the drug.[5] More than one hundred thousand "crack babies" are born each year; many are mentally retarded and physically damaged. Some of these infants also carry the AIDS virus from their mothers, who often become infected selling sex for drugs.[6]

Crack has also fueled an epidemic of drug-related crime. In the five years before crack appeared, from 1981 to 1991, violent crime in America—robbery, rape, murder, aggravated assault —fell steadily. But after the emergence of crack, violent crime exploded. From 1985 to 1991, aggravated assaults increased by over a third and robberies by 30 percent. At the same time, murders in Washington, D.C., more than doubled, while in New York City murders jumped by half.[7] By 1992, 50 to 60 percent of all those arrested in the nation's largest cities tested positive for cocaine and crack, regardless of the charge at arrest.[8]

Nor is crack the only problem. More recently, heroin use has been on the rise as well. Because of its calming effect, heroin is popular among drug addicts trying to come down from crack binges. Traditionally, heroin sold in the United States has been so diluted that it must be injected to maxmize its effect, but the heroin available today is so inexpensive and pure that it can be smoked and still provide a powerful high. Since smoking eliminates the need for needles, this "new" heroin may also attract users who have previously been discouraged by the fear of contracting AIDS.[9]

Still other drugs are on the horizon: "designer" drugs, which can be made in home laboratories from easily available chemicals; LSD and other hallucinogens, which are enjoying renewed popularity among young people nostalgic for the 1960s; smokable amphetamines such as "ice," which produce even more intense highs and lows than crack; and inhalants, like lighter fluid and paint thinner, which can be bought in any neighborhood store. We can be sure of only one thing: in the future, new products will emerge to feed America's appetite for drugs.[10] The problem will not go away. Something must be done.

■

The destructive impact of drugs on American life makes the "war on drugs" a highly charged political issue. Before every recent election politicians have outdone each other demanding tougher drug policies. Congress passed major antidrug legislation before the 1986, 1988, and 1990 elections, including large increases in funding. Since 1986, the federal drug budget has quadrupled, reaching $12.1 billion in 1994.

During this period, America's war on drugs has been shaped by the view that drug abuse is primarily a challenge to law enforcement rather than a health or social problem. Most of our antidrug tax dollars have supported programs to reduce drug supplies by going after drug producers, traffickers, and dealers. President Ronald Reagan believed that America's drug problems resulted not only from ready supplies but also from widespread tolerance of drug use. He advocated "zero tolerance" of all drugs and stepped up enforcement against both dealers and users. At the same time, he mounted a major interdiction campaign to stop the flow of drugs across our borders.

During Reagan's first term, funding for drug law enforcement more than doubled, from $800 million in 1981 to $1.9 billion in 1985, while education and treatment funds were cut from $404 million to $338 million. Attorney General Edwin Meese, head of the National Drug Policy Board, noted that the Reagan administration had created "the largest increases in drug law enforcement funding and manpower in the nation's history." The drug war was touted as a great success, and government press offices issued daily reports of drug seizures, drug arrests, and criminal convictions.

By the mid-1980s, however, it had become clear that the massive commitment of money and effort had failed. Despite record drug seizures and unprecedented numbers of arrests, drug abuse and drug-related crime soared. At the same time, the purity of street drugs rose while prices fell. In 1981 a kilogram of cocaine in Miami sold for $60,000; six years later, that same kilogram sold for $12,000. The National Narcotics Intelligence Consumers Committee reported in 1987 that cocaine was widely available at the lowest prices ever reported.[11] The strategy was not working.

Faced with a national cocaine epidemic, President Reagan admitted before the 1986 midterm elections that "all the confiscation and law enforcement in the world will not cure this plague." But the president's rhetorical bow to reality had little impact on his administration's drug strategy. During his second term, law enforcement continued to dominate policy, while prevention, education, and treatment programs received less than one-quarter of the total antidrug budget.

Not much changed under George Bush, who pledged an even bolder assault on drugs during the 1988 campaign, and declared in his inaugural address, "Take my word for it, this scourge will stop." Although antidrug funding tripled during his term, his priority remained law enforcement, which received 70 percent of the federal drug budget

And in his first year in office, President Bill Clinton continued the Bush policies. However, his proposed $13.2 billion antidrug budget for 1995 increases expenditures for treatment and prevention by $800 million, giving demand reduction and supply control equal funding for the first time in fourteen years.

■

Defining drug abuse as a law enforcement problem has long been an automatic response for politicians as they face voters alarmed by escalating rates of addiction and crime. Since 1981,

Americans have spent over $100 billion in federal, state, and local taxes to support drug enforcement programs.[12] Gauged by the traditional goals of these programs—higher drug prices and reduced availability—these efforts have been a dismal failure. Yet there has been no public inquiry into drug enforcement's effectiveness, even as the costs continue to rise. The General Accounting Office reported in 1991 that the flow of drugs into the United States had not declined despite massive expenditures for interdiction. A good example of misguided spending is the set of fourteen radar balloons currently floating above the U.S.-Mexican border and the Gulf of Mexico. At an average purchase price of $20 million each, these balloons are intended to spot suspicious airborne drug smugglers. Yet they are unable to fly in bad weather, are easily damaged, and cost $42 million a year to operate. There is no evidence that they have increased drug seizures since they first went aloft in 1986.[13]

Even under the most favorable conditions, efforts to cut off foreign drug supplies have had only a temporary effect on American drug use. This is because a relatively small volume of drugs can supply our entire drug market. A twenty-square-mile field of opium poppies produces enough heroin to meet annual American demand. Four Boeing 747 cargo planes or thirteen trailer trucks can supply American cocaine consumption for a year. Moreover, many foreign countries are capable of producing these drugs. Whenever one foreign drug source is shut down, another can rapidly replace it.[14]

The chief goal of interdiction is to increase the cost of drugs to American users, but we have learned that interdiction has very little effect on street prices. The largest profits from the drug traffic are made not in foreign poppy or coca fields or on the high seas but at the street level. Economists at the Rand Corporation estimate that only 10 percent of the final street price for cocaine goes to those who produce coca or smuggle it across the borders. Even if we were able to seize half the co-caine coming from South America—a wildly optimistic pros-pect—cocaine prices in American cities would increase by less than 5 percent.[15] With a vial of crack selling in most places for less than the cost of a single admission to the movies, such increases would not likely affect consumption.

We have learned that attacking drug addiction by trying to cut off supplies does not work and is unlikely to work in the future. Yet our government spends more for interdiction and foreign control efforts than for treatment. We continue to pur-sue a policy that cannot work.

■

Not only have we failed to reduce the supplies of illicit drugs, we have also failed to reduce the human toll of our drug prob-lem. Record numbers of arrests have not diminished violent crime, addiction, and urban blight. Unprecedented seizures have not reduced the numbers of drug-affected infants, whose care will cost the nation $2.5 billion by 1997.[16] Treatment is available for fewer than 20 percent of the nation's 5.5 million drug abusers who need help, unless they can afford to pay for private programs.[17] Drug treatment within the criminal justice system is even more limited, although two-thirds of the 1.35 million offenders currently behind bars have serious drug prob-lems.[18]

The lack of drug treatment also exacerbates the AIDS epi-demic, since sharing dirty needles is now the most rapid route for transmitting the AIDS virus in the United States. Nearly a third of all AIDS cases result from intravenous drug use, and half the nation's estimated 1.8 million intravenous drug users are at risk for HIV infection. In New York City, which has more than 200,000 heroin addicts, over half the AIDS cases between 1981 and 1993 were drug related.[19]

The progress we have made against drugs during the past decade has resulted not from reduced supply but from reduced demand. Cocaine and marijuana use has substantially declined since 1988, largely because of greater awareness of health dangers and increasingly negative social attitudes about drugs.[20] At the same time, cocaine and marijuana are readily available, suggesting that drug scarcity and high prices—the traditional measures of law enforcement success—are not responsible for the declines.

Among high school seniors, cocaine use has dropped by more than half since 1988, despite the fact that most students say they can easily obtain the drug.[21] Marijuana use, after a period of substantial decline, has begun to increase. Among all Americans age twelve and over, however, drug use has dropped steadily since 1981. More than 90 percent of the public believe that using heroin and cocaine carries great risk of harm, while three-fourths think regular marijuana use is dangerous.[22]

Progress, however, is largely limited to better educated Americans who are more inclined to respond to health information. Cocaine use declined from 1985 to 1990 almost twice as much among those who had attended college as among those who had not.[23] Teenagers who plan to continue their education after high school are also less likely to use drugs.[24] Dr. Peter Reuter, director of the Rand Corporation's Drug Policy Research Center, points out that "the deaths of sports stars Len Bias and Don Rogers riveted national attention on the dangers of cocaine. Better educated Americans who used cocaine occasionally were the first to quit."

Despite these encouraging reductions among some segments of society, the latest surveys indicate that addiction is getting worse, not better. The Office of National Drug Control Policy estimates that there are at least 2.1 million "hard-core" cocaine addicts, triple the number of earlier estimates, as well as an additional 600,000 heroin addicts.[25] Although drug use is still declining among adults, the most recent survey of high school students reports that disapproval of drug use is weakening, and that marijuana and inhalant use has increased each year since 1991. Cocaine and heroin overdose cases, as reported in hospital emergency rooms across the country, jumped 9 percent between 1992 and 1993.[26] These figures suggest that the drug epidemic is far from over.

■

It is not surprising that most Americans express deep pessimism about our ability as a nation to deal with drug abuse. Despite massive expenditures, we have not reduced either drug addiction or crime. Yet our pessimism has not compelled us to rethink our strategies, to question why we continue to rely so heavily on law enforcement and border interdiction. The apparent intractability of drug addiction has led many people to embrace extreme solutions ranging from draconian criminal sentences to outright legalization. Both are counsels of despair.

I heard the despair that "nothing works" voiced most clearly in a large Midwestern city several years ago at a meeting of business and civic leaders trying to put together a drug strategy. The publisher of the major newspaper asked, "How can we do anything if we don't know what works? We'll just have to write off this generation until someone comes up with some answers."

This book attempts to counter this despair, to show that there are programs that do work and that we ought not to give up. Over the past five years, I have visited dozens of treatment centers across the country; I have met people who are organizing their neighborhoods; I have spoken with teachers, researchers, police officials, and business leaders who are finding new approaches to preventing drug abuse and crime. While there is no single solution to this problem, many programs are making a real difference. Some can serve as models for other communities; others are harder to replicate. All of them provide answers —often in very different ways—to the question, What works?

Some programs have been more rigorously tested than others. For example, we know much more about drug education in the schools, which has been the primary focus of prevention efforts for several decades, than about organizing entire communities to combat drug dealing. But though systematic evaluation is often hard to come by in the drug field (largely because of a critical lack of resources for research during the past decade), there are encouraging indicators, such as declining local drug crime rates, which suggest that some programs are moving in the right direction.

So, too, with research on treatment. We have a long history of treating heroin addiction and a relatively short experience with crack cocaine. Yet we can already see the positive impact of some programs in reducing drug abuse and criminal activity. We have a solid practical knowledge of what works and what doesn't, and which directions we should explore further.

We know prevention must begin early, before children begin experimenting with drugs. We know they must be taught the skills to resist social pressures. We also know that even the best school prevention programs do not inoculate children against drugs for the rest of their lives. Thus successful prevention efforts must expand beyond the classroom to include the larger environment which shapes our attitudes toward drugs—families, neighborhoods, churches, businesses, the media.

We know that communities play a critically important role in combating drugs. Some communities are fighting back, organizing themselves to drive out drugs. Police departments are helping citizens reclaim their streets, keeping up pressure on dealers and working to make neighborhoods safer. Communities are also building political coalitions of business, media, and civic leaders to concentrate public attention on the drug problem and to create new strategies.

■

The overall declines in marijuana and cocaine use suggest that reducing demand for drugs is much more promising than efforts to cut off supplies. The evidence has become so compelling that senior police officials are often the strongest advocates for making demand reduction a top priority. Bruce Philpott, former chief of police of Pasadena, California, observes, "The police see every day that law enforcement alone can't solve addiction. The most we can do is show them they've reached bottom, but locking them up won't change their behavior unless they get treatment. Without a big shift in priorities—so we really go after demand—we're fighting a losing battle."

Public pressure remains high for immediate, dramatic action, even if its ultimate impact is negligible. Police sweeps of drug-infested neighborhoods that generate hundreds of new arrests are politically popular, but too often they only feed more people through the revolving doors of overcrowded courts and jails. Without longer-term efforts to reduce the market for drugs, the dealers are back on the streets within days.

Even with a strategy focused on prevention and treatment, law enforcement still has an important role to play. Many communities have discovered that sustained cooperation between neighborhood police and local residents is a better way to reduce drug availability than costly interdiction programs designed to seal the nation's borders. Confiscating automobiles, houses, and other assets involved in drug deals is often a more powerful deterrent than the threat of arrest and more attractive to hard-pressed local governments in need of revenues. These new approaches are changing lives and transforming communities, but we have not begun to apply this knowledge broadly enough. Our drug policies continue to rely on strategies which have largely failed.

Underlying these new approaches is a transformation in attitudes as individuals understand that the drug problem affects everyone and that they can do something about it. Some people are moved by personal experience of drug abuse, while others see what drugs have done to their communities. They know that the traditional supply-side assumptions about combating drug abuse are not working.

A bank executive in Miami described this transformation, which has been shared by many other communities, when he explained, "We finally realized we had to take ownership of this problem before it destroyed our city. We were losing business, and people were afraid to come here because of drug crime and violence. Meanwhile, law enforcement funding kept going up along with new federal task forces involving the DEA, Customs, and Coast Guard. But the problem kept getting worse. By 1989, we knew we could not afford to go on hoping tougher interdiction and more arrests would make a difference. Now we are creating new options which involve every major institution in this city—through the schools, the courts, on the streets and in treatment programs—and we are beginning to see real results for the first time."

■

Although drug abuse cuts across all social classes, it is far more visible among the poor, who are at much greater risk for unemployment, AIDS, homelessness, and crime. Their children are more likely to be sick, to drop out of school, or to be placed in foster care. Treatment is far less available to them than to those who have health insurance or can afford private programs.

emotional growth that strengthens a child's ability to resist. The longer the delay, the less likely it is that abuse will occur. Only 10 percent of all smokers, for example, take up the habit after the age of eighteen.[3] And for those who have already begun smoking, drinking, or using drugs, education about the dangers of these substances can keep them from becoming heavy users or even persuade them to quit.

Until recently, most prevention programs failed—in large part because they were based on faulty assumptions about why young people begin using alcohol, tobacco, and drugs in the first place.[4]

Early prevention efforts relied on scare tactics and moral exhortations, expressing prohibitionist views that linked drugs to dangerous criminal influences. *Reefer Madness*, a drug-education film made by the Federal Bureau of Narcotics after marijuana was outlawed in 1937, is a good example. The film depicts the downfall of a promising young man after one puff of marijuana. Instantly he becomes violent, abusive, and sexually aggressive, shocking his friends and his boss, and ending his chances for success. The message is clear: marijuana has transformed a son of the middle class into a crazed criminal.

Although the film reflected prevailing American attitudes in the 1940s and 1950s, when illicit drug use remained low, scare tactics failed completely to stop the wave of new marijuana use that swept across America in the 1960s. Instead of frightening young people, such efforts served only to prove that adults either did not know what they were talking about or were prepared to lie to force conformist behavior on young people. Millions of teenagers stopped believing negative messages about drugs, and *Reefer Madness* became a cult film among young drug users.

Faced with a complete loss of credibility, prevention efforts turned next to providing straight information about drugs, including their pharmacology, psychological effects, and health hazards, as well as about the legal consequences of getting caught. These programs targeted high school students, the age at which drug use then began. Students learned about drugs much as they learned history—from teachers' lectures and limited classroom discussion. Some programs continued to blend scare tactics with more solid information, on the assumption that young people use drugs because they do not believe they are dangerous. Once made fully aware of the risks, the thinking went, they would stop using drugs. While many of these programs increased teenagers' knowledge about drugs they had no appreciable impact on drug use. In fact, they sometimes stimulated students' curiosity, tempting, even challenging them to try the high-risk lives they were told so many of their peers were living.

In the 1970s the focus of prevention moved away from drug use and concentrated on the personality of the individual drug user. These programs were based on the view that young people use drugs because of personal problems—low self-esteem, poor communication skills, and inability to make decisions. Programs were designed to improve the student's self-image and ability to relate to others, emphasizing values, feelings, and self-awareness, often without any reference to drugs. Students were taught how to identify social problems, create solutions, and choose among alternatives.

Few of these "affective education" programs were systematically evaluated, but those that were failed to show reduced drug use among the students in the programs. The programs did not relate improved communication and decision-making skills to drug use, so that teenagers still did not know what to do when a friend offered them marijuana. Even programs that did succeed in improving the students' self-esteem could not be demonstrated to have reduced drug use.

By the early 1980s, however, prevention programs began to reflect a broader understanding of the factors influencing young adolescents to try drugs. This "social influences" model views drug use as something children learn from their environment. Drug use begins not because children lack information or have personality problems, but because they are especially vulnerable in preteen years to social pressures. In their desire to be accepted, youngsters tend to copy behavior they consider adult, including drinking, smoking, and using drugs.[5]

Prevention programs now target younger children, concentrating on the sixth and seventh grades, when they begin experimenting with alcohol, tobacco, and drugs. At this stage, they are still eager to learn resistance skills. Moreover, children remain a captive audience in these earlier grades. In many cities, more than half the class will have dropped out by the time they reach high school.

The "social influences" approach to teaching prevention is very different from earlier efforts. Information about alcohol, drugs, and tobacco is still provided, but in ways young adolescents will react to more directly. Emphasis now is on short-term negative effects, rather than on more abstract long-term dangers. For eleven- and twelve-year-olds the fact that smoking makes their breath smell bad is a more powerful deterrent than the fear of lung cancer. As one drug-prevention teacher in a San Francisco elementary school said, "It's often hard for us to remember that at that age, you think you really would rather die than have the other kids laugh at you. Social rejection is much more frightening than the seemingly remote possibility of death."

The goal is to help children understand the pressures they feel to use tobacco, alcohol, and drugs, and to teach them how to resist these pressures. Many children smoke, drink, and use drugs to relieve anxiety or to fit in socially, because they assume that "everybody's doing it." Adolescents often overestimate the extent of drug use and rarely discuss this with each other. Advertising reinforces their assumptions by promoting images of successful, popular young people who smoke and drink. Teaching adolescents to recognize how advertising tries to manipulate their behavior helps them examine all packaged messages more critically.[6] Reviewing national drug use surveys or having students organize their own school surveys is also helpful. In fact, only a quarter of sixth- and seventh-graders nationwide have tried alcohol, one-fifth have tried smoking, and fewer than 3 percent have used marijuana.[7]

These new programs also give children explicit strategies for refusing tobacco, alcohol, and drugs without fear of rejection. Because peer pressure rarely takes the form of direct solicitation, children are not often presented with a clear opportunity to "just say no." Instead, they find themselves in a group where others are engaging in these activities and they feel driven to conform. Learning how to avoid these situations, or to get out of them gracefully, gives them skills to rely on when the time comes.

Life Skills Training (LST), designed in the late 1970s by Dr. Gilbert J. Botvin at Cornell University Medical College in New York City, is one of the most promising programs built on the "social influences" approach. LST teaches children how to make decisions, solve problems, and handle broader social relations so that they feel more confident. LST assumes that if youngsters have more ways to achieve their goals, they will be less likely to turn to tobacco, alcohol, and drugs. To do this, seventh-graders learn personal coping skills in a fifteen-session curriculum—how to deal with anxiety through deep-breathing exercises, how to overcome shyness in a social group, as well as how to resist pressures that come from advertising and from other youngsters. In addition, LST gives students accurate information on current levels of alcohol, tobacco, and drug use among adolescents.

Gloria Williams, who has taught LST to predominantly black and Hispanic seventh-graders in New York City, explains, "The idea is to help kids feel more confident so they won't think they have to use drugs to fit in. We practice really basic skills, like starting a conversation, smiling when you see someone you know, and how to act when someone is rude to you. Many kids haven't been taught to be polite; they are used to being aggressive, so it's hard for them to feel comfortable in social situations. They really get involved in these sessions, and like to practice in the safety of the classroom. They want to learn how to be more in control."

LST has been rigorously evaluated in 150 junior high schools in New York and New Jersey over the past decade. Four-year follow-up studies report that rates of smoking and marijuana use are one-half to three-quarters lower among students who have participated in LST than among those who have not. LST also reduces alcohol use, although not as substantially, and the effects are sometimes inconsistent. For example, one study found that declines in student drinking reported immediately after the program had disappeared two years later, while another study found a "sleeper" effect which produced significant reductions six months after students participated in LST.[8]

Nonetheless, LST consistently reports positive results in reducing problem drinking. Even after LST graduates begin using alcohol, they generally consume less than other students, and by ninth and tenth grade, LST graduates report substantially less drunkenness than other students.

■

STAR (Students Taught Awareness and Resistance), developed in the early 1980s at the University of Southern California's Institute for Health Promotion and Disease Prevention Research, is one of the most effective prevention programs in the country. Like LST, STAR is built on the social influences approach, but STAR combines classroom teaching with a larger strategy involving the family, the media, and the community.

As part of the STAR curriculum, children take home assignments to work on with their parents, assignments designed to open up family discussions on drugs and alcohol. Michael Herman, the former president of the Kauffman Foundation in Kansas City, which supports STAR, recounted that doing the STAR homework with his own children was an eye-opener. "We all like to think we communicate well with our kids," he said, "but when we went through that material together, I saw I hadn't worked out my own attitudes toward alcohol. I just knew I didn't want them copying me and my friends, and that meant changing my drinking habits."

In Kansas City, STAR's classroom and family programs are reinforced by media campaigns, and sports and recreational activities which emphasize the importance and social desirability of not using drugs. In addition, a coalition of civic leaders, businesspeople, and government officials works together to concentrate community resources on combating substance abuse. Special working groups explore ways to make tobacco and alcohol less available to minors, particularly through better monitoring at convenience stores and other outlets near schools.

STAR teaches resistance skills to students in the first year of middle school through a twelve-session curriculum which focuses on correcting students' misperceptions of the prevalence of drug use and helps them recognize media, family, and peer influences. Students are encouraged to talk about their positive and negative perceptions of alcohol, tobacco, and drugs as well as the consequences of using these substances. Through role playing, they are able to practice how to respond in different situations where they might feel social pressures to participate. A five-session booster program is taught the following year to reinforce their skills.

■

The Argentine Middle School is located in a working-class suburb of Kansas City. The long one-story brick buildings are clean and cheerful. In one of the classrooms, twenty-four sixth-grade students have just begun the STAR program. Their teacher, Vicki Estrada, has been teaching STAR since the program began in 1984. Her energy and enthusiasm fill the room as she asks the class to write down the names of six people who influence them.

A small girl at a table in the front of the room timidly raises her hand and asks what "influence" means. Estrada tosses the question back to the class. One boy calls out, "Someone who tells me how to act." The boy next to him adds, "Someone I want to be like." Estrada asks them to give examples. The first boy says, "My older brother." Estrada walks over to his table and asks with a smile, "How about your teacher? She better influence you!" The children laugh and clap their hands.

She divides the class into four groups and asks them to think about a specific situation. "You've been invited to ride home with a friend. His older brother, who is the captain of the high school football team, is driving, and has two teammates with him. On the way home, he says, 'Let's stop and have a joint. It won't take long. Don't worry, I won't tell.' What are three negative things and three positive things that would happen if you agree?"

Each group talks noisily. Estrada walks around the

classroom calming down some of the children, encouraging others to write down a response. After fifteen minutes, the class reassembles and each group reports. A slender black boy, whose hair is carefully clipped to spell "NIKE," says that if they get high they might have an accident and miss the game that night. A girl near him jumps up and says, "My mom was furious when my big brother came in drunk last week and threw him out of the house." Another girl joins in, "You could get in real trouble. My mom's boyfriend was caught with drugs and now he's in jail."

Estrada asks them what positive things might happen if they smoke the joint. A tall blond boy calls out, "It could be a lot of fun." A boy from another group waves his hand and says, "The older guys will think you're cool. Maybe I'd get to hang out with them after games." Estrada asks the other children whether they agree. Most don't, pointing out the negative consequences of smoking marijuana. Estrada leads them through a discussion of other ways to have fun and be socially accepted, making sure they all participate.

The bell rings and Estrada dismisses the class for recess. She tells them that next week they will each get to act out the situation they have discussed today, so they should be thinking about it.

Estrada likes the STAR program and says that drug use is declining at Argentine Middle School. She explains, "What we do in this class is different from our other work. We're not just giving them knowledge, we're trying to change their behavior so they will be able and willing to resist drugs. We spend a lot of time practicing what to say and how to act in these situations, because otherwise many of them will go along with what the other kids in the group are doing." Putting on her coat to go out to the playground, Estrada adds, with a smile, "That sounds like a tall order for a teacher to pull off, but compared to six years ago when we began this program, the kids are getting antidrug messages everywhere—on TV, radio, when they go to games. It's not just my voice they hear anymore. The whole atmosphere is different, and that makes what we do in class easier."

■

STAR has trained teachers in over 400 middle and junior high schools in Kansas and Missouri and 97 schools in Indianapolis, and has been recently introduced in over 30 schools in Washington, D.C. Comprehensive evaluations of STAR since 1984 have reported significant results in preventing smoking, drinking, and drug use, in both inner-city and affluent schools. Five-year follow-up studies involving 5,500 students report that rates of tobacco, marijuana, and alcohol use among children who had participated in STAR were 20 to 40 percent lower than among those who had not. However, the average reductions in drinking were only half as great as those for smoking and marijuana use.[9] By ninth and tenth grade, STAR graduates used cocaine at half the rate of other students.[10]

Evaluations of STAR's comprehensive approach in Kansas City indicate that the classroom program is the key factor in the effectiveness of STAR's larger environmental strategy. Without high-quality prevention teaching, STAR's media and community prevention efforts have little impact on adolescent drug and alcohol use.[11]

Dr. Mary Ann Pentz, a leading prevention researcher who helped design STAR, thinks the value of the comprehensive community approach lies in changing social attitudes about drug use. "STAR graduates are more able to resist the intense pressures to use drugs when they get to high school, not only because they have the skills but because they find support at home and in the community," Pentz explains. "The fact that STAR graduates use cocaine at only half the rate of other ninth- and tenth-grade students shows the power of social attitudes in shaping teenagers' behavior. There's a much stronger consensus now against cocaine than before, and that's magnifying the prevention effect we get from classroom teaching."

As LST and STAR evaluations have found, alcohol is more resistant to prevention efforts than tobacco and drugs. This is not surprising, given the central importance of social attitudes in influencing children's drug use. Children bring society's values with them into the classroom, and it is far easier for youngsters to resist tobacco and marijuana, which are now widely stigmatized, than it is to resist drinking, which is seen in a more favorable light all around them. Even among teenagers—for whom alcohol is illegal—the prevailing norm is to drink. Nationwide, 39 percent of youngsters aged twelve to seventeen reported drinking in 1992. By the time they are seniors, three-quarters of all high school students will drink.[12]

Dr. Linda Dusenbury, who helped develop Life Skills Training, points out, "There is real disagreement in this country about whether we should be teaching abstinence or responsible use of alcohol, even to junior high school students. Kids that young can't make sophisticated decisions about drinking; they need to have a clear message. But even if a prevention program teaches abstinence, everyone around them—their friends, families, and community—and the constant barrage of advertising seem to encourage drinking. Overcoming these social attitudes may be too heavy a burden for schools to carry alone." To change drinking behavior significantly among the young will require a broad national effort to modify public attitudes toward alcohol, including more restrictions on advertising, tighter controls on where alcohol can be sold, and more active en-forcement of the drinking-age laws.[13]

Moreover, the gains achieved with the social-influences ap-proach fade as sixth- and seventh-graders move through high school. The social pressures to drink, smoke, and use drugs become more intense during these years. LST booster sessions in eighth and ninth grade reinforce the skills learned in earlier years, and result in larger reductions in marijuana and tobacco use. STAR does not provide boosters beyond eighth grade, but reduced high school cocaine use among STAR graduates suggests that a more comprehensive approach involving fami-lies and the community may help reinforce earlier prevention learning.

Even prevention programs that have proved successful else-where are not readily adopted in many public schools. Overbur-dened administrators are often reluctant to assume additional responsibilities. Trying to reduce drug use through special vid-eos and guest speakers may seem easier than making a commit-ment to a lengthy curriculum. Teachers also may not want to take time away from academic subjects and may feel uncomfort-able dealing with drug use, even if they have received special training.

Resistance within the school system has led to the wide-spread popularity of programs like DARE (Drug Abuse Resis-tance Education), which is now taught to more than 5 million children in every state in the country. Uniformed police offi-cers teach prevention in the final year of elementary school, usually fifth or sixth grade. Relying on outsiders relieves the schools from having to give up their own teachers for preven-tion training, hire substitutes, and administer the program. But studies have shown that DARE does not reduce tobacco, alcohol, or drug use. Using police officers tends to divorce prevention from the students' daily learning, and regular classroom teachers are unlikely to reinforce the material in their own classes.[14]

Many schools rely on programs which have not been evaluated or, worse yet, have been found to have no impact. In 1988 a review of 350 different school programs found that only 33 had any valid evaluation data, while just 3 programs reported reductions in tobacco, alcohol, or drug use. The study concluded that the only apparent function of the other 347 programs was "reassurance of parents that the schools are at least trying to control substance abuse among students."[15]

In 1994 the Department of Education provided $469 million nationwide for school drug and violence prevention programs; local districts can use their own allotments with no strings attached.[16] Administrators faced with a bewildering variety of choices often buy the package that is marketed most aggressively. The U.S. Department of Education, reluctant to endorse any curriculum, sent its own prevention model to every school district in the country in 1990, even though it had never been evaluated. A senior Bush administration drug policy official observed at the time, "We need an independent group to establish a consumer's guide to the best prevention programs so that schools won't pour their money into curricula that don't work. It's not only the Colombian cartel that's gotten rich off drugs; a lot of the curriculum marketers are making out like bandits."

■

While there is no ideal blueprint for a school prevention program, we have learned in the past decade that certain elements are essential. Credible information is important, not only about the dangers of alcohol, tobacco, and drugs but also about their immediate effects. Correcting the exaggerations about almost universal drug use among peers undercuts the perception that "everyone is doing it," and frees the youngster from thinking he must smoke, drink, or take drugs to be socially accepted. Teaching children practical strategies for resisting drugs helps them handle various situations in which they find themselves under pressure to use. Active involvement of the students in the program and with each other through role playing and other dynamic classroom exercises strengthens group support for not using drugs. Family and community participation in prevention reinforces negative attitudes about drugs.

Prevention researchers believe that the social influences programs provide important gains to build on. Dr. William Hansen of Wake Forest University, who conducted a nationwide review of school prevention curricula in 1990, says, "The kind of methodological rigor we would like to see in scientific studies cannot exist in this field, because it's impossible to have perfect control over the setting—it's not like studying rats in a laboratory. But there are a number of strong evaluations that teach us something about where to go next."[17] Dr. Gilbert J. Botvin, who continues to evaluate LST, concurs: "We now have a large number of rigorous studies which show that the new approaches are effective. This pattern of success—where different researchers in different settings come up with similar findings—is powerful evidence that we're heading in the right direction."

But experts agree that prevention programs should be more comprehensive. As Dr. Mary Ann Pentz points out, "It's just not realistic to think that school programs delivered at one point in time can permanently overcome the enormous, continuing social pressure to use alcohol and drugs. We have to develop booster sessions for older children, and to think about extending drug prevention from kindergarten through high school. And for high-risk children, strategic intervention may be necessary beginning at very young ages."

■

In one of New York City's oldest public elementary schools, Eileen Wasow from the Bank Street College of Education is testing an entirely different approach for very young children—a program known as Project Healthy Choices. The Upper West Side neighborhood is poor and predominantly Hispanic. A security guard stationed inside the school's front hall asks visitors for identification, which he checks against names on a list.

Before leading a visitor into the classroom, Wasow explains why Project Healthy Choices is needed. "Social denial of substance abuse is very strong, even in neighborhoods like this where crack deals happen every day. This program helps teachers and kids talk openly about what they see and experience. In most classrooms, teachers don't encourage this kind of discussion, because they're afraid the parents or the administration will be upset. And they don't know how to talk about it comfortably."

Asked whether five- and six-year-olds are ready to discuss drug and alcohol abuse, Wasow answers emphatically, "They sure are! We carry a lot of mythology about protecting young kids. But our kids see parents using and dealing drugs. Adults don't speak to kids about any of this. Just because a child isn't talking about it doesn't mean he doesn't see it."

Nancy Klein, one of the Bank Street trainers who is working with the teachers in this school, adds, "We're not talking about preventing five-year-olds from taking drugs today or tomorrow, because they're not about to use, even in the worst neighborhoods. We're trying to get them talking about the reality of their lives and help them see they have choices.

"We also work with the parents. We speak to them about the mixed messages our kids get from watching our behavior and listening to our words. The parents go through the same interactive process with the kids that the teachers are going through in the classes. It's hard to get all the parents to participate, but we are getting some."

The bell rings, and Klein and Wasow climb steep stone steps to a classroom on the third floor. Klein has just started working with this class and will meet later with the regular teacher to go over what has happened that day. She carries teaching materials developed for Project Healthy Choices, a videotape and a storybook which can be used to stimulate discussion. She explains, "We look for the teachable moment. We want to help teachers raise open-ended questions which integrate children's thinking and feeling. We encourage them to bring their concerns into class in a safe way and help them talk about what's going on. Our main goal is to strengthen their growth and help them resist drugs and alcohol."

The crowded classroom is sunny, filled with plants and art construction projects. The children are in uniforms as part of a campaign to increase pride in inner-city schools. The girls wear plaid jumpers over white blouses; the boys, cardigan sweaters with the school emblem on the pocket. Eager to begin, the children gather in a circle on the floor around Klein. Their teacher sits nearby and translates when one of them can't find the words in English.

"Does anybody know what a family is?" Klein asks. A girl with long brown pigtails jumps up, waves her hand, and bursts out, "A mama, and sisters, and cousins, and grandmas, and grandpas." Another girl adds, "Brothers, too, and dogs, and sometimes cats."

"What about daddies?" Klein asks. The children nod and

murmur. A chubby boy whose cardigan barely stretches across his stomach says, "My daddy isn't there too much. He goes out and drinks beers. When he comes home, he beats up my mommy. My big sister says he's sick. I asked him to stop but he says he can't."

"Who remembers what we talked about last time? What should José say to his dad?" Klein says, turning to the girl sitting next to her. "He should go to the doctor or to a hospital to get well," she answers.

Klein asks, "Can someone tell us what a hospital is?" A red-haired boy says shyly in Spanish, "If someone gets killed and the mommy starts crying, they call the hospital." The teacher translates for him.

"The hospital or clinic is where you go to get help when you're hurt or sick," Klein explains. "Drinking too much and taking drugs can make you really sick."

A solemn-looking girl in glasses says, "My dad got drunk a lot, and then he went to a rehab clinic and got better." The teacher asks the class if they would like to construct a model clinic before Klein comes again. They clap enthusiastically.

Klein takes out an oversized picture storybook and tells them she has a few minutes to read to them. The story recounts the efforts of a wily alley cat named Slippery Slick to persuade the good little Clever Kitten to sneak out of school and try a cigarette. The children listen intently, sometimes looking to their teacher for help with English.

Klein asks them, "What was Slippery doing?" José says, "Trying to trick the other cat into doing something not nice."

The girl sitting next to him adds, "Slippery is trying to get the kitten into trouble." Klein smiles at them, "You're both right. Next time we'll talk about the story again. Do you have your own stories like that?" Many of the children nod. They groan when Klein gets up to leave. Several plead for her to stay longer. She promises to return next week.

■

Project Healthy Choices has been enthusiastically accepted in one hundred New York City schools, where it was initially evaluated in 1990.[18] The study found that participating teachers feel better able to talk about drugs and alcohol. They strongly favor weaving prevention into everyday teaching—it keeps them from having to choose between a separate prevention curriculum and regular classroom subjects. Future evaluations will test the impact the program is having on the children.

Although we will have a better idea about the effectiveness of Project Healthy Choices as further studies are done, the critical importance of sustained, high-quality teaching is already apparent. Project Healthy Choices gives teachers ownership of the program by training them to introduce discussions about drugs and alcohol into their daily activities. This integration reinforces the children's learning about drugs across a range of academic subjects and multiplies the "teachable moment" throughout the school year.

Dr. Cal Cormack, a former high school principal who directs the STAR program nationwide, thinks the Bank Street model may be the wave of the future. "We give up time from other subjects in sixth and seventh grade to teach prevention because we know that kids won't learn anything at all if they're using drugs and alcohol," Cormack explains. "But if we could break down the traditional divisions between prevention and academic teaching beginning in kindergarten, we might be able to achieve larger, more sustained results."

The Bank Street program creates a new classroom climate

where drug and alcohol problems are discussed more openly than in the past. Very young students are taught that they are not at fault if their parents get drunk or sell drugs. They also learn that they do not have to act that way themselves. Understanding how to make healthy choices about drugs and alcohol is important for all children, but for those whose circumstances put them at particularly high risk for substance abuse, this new approach may prove invaluable.

4
■

Helping High-Risk Kids

' No children are immune to substance abuse. They are all vulnerable to drugs and alcohol, whether they live in poor, inner-
city neighborhoods surrounded by addicts and dealers, or in
wealthy suburbs where these problems are better hidden. But
some children—as many as seven million aged ten to seventeen
—are at especially high risk because of their personal and family circumstances.[1]

   We cannot predict with certainty which children will become substance abusers, but we know a good deal about the
factors which increase the likelihood of later problems. Substance abuse by a parent is a very strong predictor. So is a
lack of parental guidance or a disruptive home without clear,
consistent rules. Early experimentation with drugs increases
the risk of later abuse. So does living in a community where
substance abuse and dealing are pervasive. A history of aca-

demic failure and rebellious, antisocial behavior in elementary school is linked to later problems with drugs as well as to truancy, delinquency, and early pregnancy.

While these risk factors are all important predictors, the effect of any one alone can be muted by other circumstances in a child's life. However, two risk factors produce four times the probability of problem behaviors. Children facing multiple risks are much more likely to move from experimentation to serious substance abuse by the time they are teenagers.[2]

The most effective school prevention programs set out to reduce some of these risk factors by teaching children skills to resist pressures to smoke, drink, and take drugs. Although LST and STAR do well in both inner-city and suburban classrooms, they are not designed specifically for high-risk children. As STAR's Dr. Mary Ann Pentz points out, "For high-risk children, extra efforts are needed. We are just beginning to recognize the importance of 'strategic' prevention for particularly vulnerable children. The increasing acceptance of primary prevention makes it easier for adults and children to recognize who might be at special risk and reduces the stigma attached to seeking help."

The risks of developing drug and alcohol problems increase as children enter high school. The transition from junior high school can be difficult as young teenagers move from a smaller, more structured environment to larger institutions where they quickly feel lost. Unlike the earlier grades, the dominant culture in high school tolerates, and often encourages, smoking, drinking, and using drugs. Nationwide, a quarter of all tenth-graders have tried illegal drugs, over half have smoked, and eight out of ten have tried alcohol.[3] In recent years, "Let's party" has come to mean "Let's go get drunk" for many teenagers. Concerned parents and schools have established safe-ride programs for students who have been drinking, as well as alternative alcohol-free and drug-free parties. But apart from these efforts, very few prevention programs target high school students.

■

The Westchester Student Assistance Program (SAP) offers one of the most promising approaches to preventing teenage substance abuse. SAP provides counseling to students during the school day on a voluntary, confidential basis. Most of the participants are at high risk for drug and alcohol problems: about two-thirds are children of substance abusers or are themselves already drinking and using drugs. SAP's goal is to prevent substance abuse as well as improve the youngster's ability to function in school and at home.

SAP began as an experiment in 1979, when Ellen Morehouse, a social worker in an adolescent counseling program in Westchester County, New York, got tired of waiting in her office for school referrals. "We weren't reaching teenagers until they'd gotten into really serious trouble," Morehouse recalls. "I decided to take drug and alcohol counseling into the schools to make it as easy as possible for kids to get help on their own, sometimes before they even knew they had a problem. Our counselors tell kids that they can come in for anything they think might lead to using drugs and alcohol. At first, they usually talk about parents or friends or sex, but alcohol and drugs are always right beneath the surface."

■

Woodacres High School is located in one of the wealthiest sections of Westchester County north of New York City. Ducks swim on a small lake near the campus entrance. Flower beds line the drive leading to the redbrick buildings housing the classrooms. The parking lot is filled with expensive cars, many of them owned by students. Jill B., a social worker trained in adolescent development, has worked with the Student Assistance Program since it began in 1979. Her office is in a small building just off the parking lot, detached from the rest of the high school. She welcomes a group of ninth-grade girls waiting outside for their weekly session. The girls are casually dressed in faded jeans, unlaced sneakers, and oversize jackets. Joking and laughing, they settle into the couches that fill Mrs. B.'s small office.

Mrs. B. asks whether anyone has the "Monday morning oh-no's," which often happen after the girls remember what they did when high or drunk at weekend parties. Sally L., a pretty fourteen-year-old, says earnestly, "I was really good. I think it's stupid to get plastered and throw up all over the place. You should be able to control yourself."

Two of the girls immediately shout at her, "Come on, Sally, you just don't remember. You were upstairs fooling around with Tom and Larry, acting like you didn't know anything."

Sally blushes and begins to bite her fingernails. "Well, at least I wasn't falling over drunk." she responds. "Last year I was drinking every day and doing pot. It got really expensive. I haven't done pot for two months." The girls cheer and Sally, smiling, raises her fist in salute.

Monica F., sitting next to her, says, "I went out with some older guys on Saturday and we smoked some pot. It was great being high, feeling so free. My parents would be furious, but I know they smoked pot when they were young."

"Do you think maybe they've learned something they hope will help you?" Mrs. B. asks.

"If they're anything like my parents," Sally bursts in, "they don't want to know anything about it."

Mrs. B. asks the girls whether they feel pressure from their friends to drink and use drugs. Ashley M., a slender blonde almost hidden in a blue Irish sweater, answers, "In sixth or seventh grade, we'd go out and get drunk on weekends. It was fun, but it was also a big deal. Now, no one cares if you drink. At parties, nobody says, 'Here, have a drink.' It's just that everybody does it, so you feel more comfortable carrying a beer can or something. And most of the kids drink to get drunk." The girls nod in agreement. "Besides, then you can do whatever you want, fool around with guys, and say you didn't know what you were doing, like it doesn't really count," Ashley adds, putting her arm around Sally.

The girls laugh, and Mrs. B. reminds them that they have all told similar stories about themselves. She asks them to think about how they can help each other at parties so they won't feel they have to get drunk or stoned. She also suggests that they might consider going to some of the drug-free parties organized by students who have pledged not to use drugs and alcohol. Sally says, "I used to think they were all geeks and nerds, just interested in grades, but some of them are cool, like Tim, who's on the varsity basketball team, and his friend Joe. I hear they go to those parties."

The bell rings and the girls gather up their things. Kathleen P., a freckled redhead who had not spoken during the session, says on her way out, "We would die without Mrs. B. She's the only person we can talk to honestly. My parents get hysterical if they even hear the word *drug*. Besides, they're never around."

After the girls leave, Jill B. explains that they have all volunteered for the program, and only the school principal knows who attends. Although most of the girls have told their mothers and fathers that they are seeing the school's SAP counselor, very few parents call to talk with her.

"Denial is the biggest obstacle we face," the counselor

says. "Our goal is to help students recognize the serious threat they face from drugs and alcohol and then motivate them to do something about it. These kids are at real risk of messing up their lives.

"In spite of what people think, these problems visit affluent families as much as poorer ones," she adds. "A lot of the parents used drugs when they were younger, and some probably still do. They all drink. But most of them don't see alcohol as a problem. As long as their kids are making good grades, they don't pay much attention to what they're doing with the rest of their time."

■

In the past decade, the Westchester Student Assistance Program has been replicated in junior and senior high schools across twenty states. A 1983 study reported that Westchester SAP reduced drinking by half and marijuana use by three-quarters among students who had participated in the program. In 1989 a comparison of Westchester high schools found that rates of drinking and drug use were one-third lower among students at schools which offered SAP. This suggests that SAP has a ripple effect beyond its participants, reducing overall use within a school.[4]

A nationwide review of ninety-one prevention programs in 1992 found Westchester SAP one of the most effective for high-risk adolescents, in large part because it deals with alcohol and drugs in the broader context of adolescent development and hires highly trained health professionals who have master's degrees and at least two years prior experience working with adolescents.[5]

Many adolescent programs fail because they are based on adult models which do not take into account the realities of adolescence. "A key concern for most adolescents is proving their power, particularly in relation to adults. That's why many people feel uncomfortable dealing with teenagers," Ellen Morehouse explains. "When we offer to help them, we do it in a way that lets them keep their power. They want to think they're unique, and we try above all else to respect their individuality. We believe that our group sessions are *their* place, and they have control. We are there to help them understand what their real problem is and what they can do to change."

Westchester SAP is popular with school principals and teachers because it provides professional assistance directly to students who need help. SAP counselors are supervised by their own independent agency as well as the high school principal. Schools usually pay at least part of the annual cost of one counselor, which ranges from $25,000 to $55,000, depending on location.

Ed Hart has been the principal at Horace Greeley High School in Chappaqua, New York, for twenty-three years. He believes that SAP has been invaluable in helping reduce student drug and alcohol problems. "Students feel safe going to Amy," he says, referring to the school's SAP counselor. "They go to her for all kinds of problems, like breaking up with a boyfriend, or being worried about leaving home to go to college. If she can't help them, she refers them somewhere that can. Parents like the idea that their kids are getting help from someone not connected to the school who doesn't make decisions about their future. Many parents are very sensitive about having their dirty linen washed in public."

Westchester SAP counselors work with parents to inform them about the risks their children face from alcohol and drugs and to help them deal more effectively with their children's problems. They organize task forces of parents, teachers, police, and local residents to change community practices, such as persuading convenience stores near schools to stop selling beer to minors. They work with teachers and students to develop consistent rules and a clear no-use message about alcohol and drugs.

Many schools no longer permit adult alcohol use at school events, and severely restrict or prohibit smoking by teachers and students. "If we're going to convince kids that they don't have to drink to have fun, we can't have parents getting high at tailgate parties before high school football games," Ellen Morehouse says.

Community attitudes are critically important in shaping adolescents' behavior. Within the more contained environment of the school, policies on alcohol, tobacco, and drugs that govern both adults and students can powerfully reinforce students' resistance to substance abuse.

In 1988 Westchester SAP expanded to six residential facilities in Westchester County for abused and delinquent children. Most are black and Hispanic, poor, and the children of substance abusers. A preliminary evaluation in 1990 found substantial declines in alcohol and drug use among children in half the facilities with much smaller declines in the rest.[6]

Ellen Morehouse believes that the SAP approach can help very high-risk children. "Adolescents use alcohol and drugs to medicate themselves when they feel anxious or stressed or afraid they won't fit in," she explains. "In the Westchester schools, kids are under a lot of pressure to excel. In these facilities, kids are under other kinds of pressure. The basic problems of development are the same, even though the external circumstances are obviously very different. The abused and delinquent children come from nonfunctional families, so we can't work with the parents the way we do in the high school program. But in both situations, our job is to help the youngsters see they can stop relying on alcohol and drugs and change the direction of their lives."

In New York City, the LST curriculum has been adapted for

children ages nine to fourteen who are living in homeless shelters, where a recent study found that 30 percent of the adults are substance abusers. Dr. Linda Dusenbury, who is directing the project, believes that teaching these children life skills is critical: "Their lives are so disrupted that it's hard for them to learn at school, and they often don't attend regularly. In the shelters, they are surrounded by substance abuse. They need to know that there are other options and they need to have the skills to help them fight anxiety and hopelessness as well as drugs and alcohol."

But Dr. Dusenbury thinks that larger social programs are also needed to provide real alternatives. "Pulling yourself up by your bootstraps is no longer possible in many areas," she explains. "Positive alternatives like decent education, jobs, health care, and housing are key to long-term prevention efforts. But teaching children life skills, even while they are in shelters, can increase their resistance to substance abuse as well as other pressures pushing them into early pregnancy, truancy, and delinquency."

■

Smart Moves is one of the few prevention curricula designed specifically for very high-risk children. Built on the social influences model, Smart Moves tailors its program for Boys and Girls Clubs in inner-city neighborhoods. Children participate in after-school prevention classes as well as in recreational, educational, and vocational activities. Like STAR, Smart Moves approaches prevention comprehensively, working at the individual, family, and community level to change attitudes about alcohol and drugs. An evaluation in 1987 reported that boys who participated in Smart Moves were more able to refuse marijuana and cocaine and less willing to try drugs than other boys.[7]

Ron Britt, assistant director of the Boys and Girls Club on

New York City's Lower East Side, likes Smart Moves because it involves the community in shaping the program. "A lot of prevention programs are directed toward affluent communities where kids are supposed to be blank slates. Here we've got junkies, crack vials, dealers on every street corner—there's no way our kids could avoid drugs," Britt explains. "We've adapted the curriculum to reflect our reality and we see good results. Smart Moves teaches kids how to recognize pressures to use drugs, how to talk with other people, how to deal with tough situations. The kids who can't verbalize usually have problems saying no, because the other kids can always outtalk them. We spend a lot of time practicing what to say and how to act when someone offers you drugs or wants you to sell some."

■

In Pompano, Florida, the Boys and Girls Club is in a one-story brick building in the poorest section of town. The large recreation room is cheerful, filled with plants, couches, and pool tables. Personal computers donated by a local business line one wall. Several hundred children come each day for sports, bingo, arts and crafts, and help with homework.

Susan Ayres, a recreational therapist who has been teaching Smart Moves for a year, is working this afternoon with eight boys on "Start Smart," the curriculum segment designed for younger children. Most of the boys come from single-parent families and live in nearby housing projects.

"I came here because I wanted to work with children, but I was scared to death at first," Ayres explains. "I'd never seen inner-city kids, and I thought they all carried knives. I didn't know how needy they would be for affection, for guidance, and how open they are to learning.

In some ways, this club becomes a family for them where there are adults they can count on."

The boys greet Ayres eagerly, crowding around to tell her what they've done in the week since they saw her. She settles them around a long table and asks if they have used any of the skills they learned in the last session. Troy L., a lively eight-year-old wearing a Miami Dolphins jacket, says, "One of my friends at school tried to get me to drink beer. He had it in his thermos. But I gave him the cold shoulder and walked away. It worked real good."

Another boy volunteers, "When I be going to church with my grandmother last Sunday, we be seeing dope dealers, a lot of them. They be selling crack and drugs, and the police just be driving along. There be a guy on the corner smoking rocks in the end of a little silver pipe, and he started shouting at me to come over. I told my granny, 'Just ignore them guys, they be no good.' "

Ayres praises both boys and asks Troy to demonstrate the cold-shoulder technique with Willie L., his much taller older brother. Willie jumps up and says to Troy, "Hey, man, don't be a chicken, try some of this crack I got here." Troy responds, "No, man, I got to go to track practice," turns his back on Willie, and walks away. The other boys cheer, and plead to take a turn, too.

Ayres reminds them to try out situations with different kinds of pressure—friendly, insulting (like calling Troy a chicken), or angry and threatening. They pair off and practice, commenting on each other's performances.

After they sit down again, Elbert M., a nine-year-old who has been silently sucking his thumb, leans forward and says, "I know a kid, his brother make him sell drugs, and now he's in detention center. He say they got drugs in there, too. They threaten you a lot. They be selling drugs in front of my Aunty Bee's house and they say they're going to come and get you and burn the place down."

Ayres puts her arm around Elbert, and Willie says, "You know they all be saying things like that but don't going to happen." Ayres adds, "The cold shoulder helps you walk away. You don't want to be aggressive and shout back because they might hurt you." Troy calls out, "They got guns and could shoot you."

Derrick P., wearing a DARE T-shirt from his school drug-prevention class, says excitedly, "The other night there was a big drug bust. My grandmother about had a heart attack when they ran into her yard. They started shooting and I cried, 'Hit the ground, Charlie!' to my little brother. I crawled into the back of the house, turned off the lights, and lay on the floors until they be gone." Ayres praises him for reacting calmly and for protecting his brother.

Ayres asks the boys if they would like to play the baseball game. The boys respond enthusiastically, jumping out of their chairs to divide into two teams, the Mets and the Yankees. She gives each team questions about drugs and alcohol and they work together to come up with an answer.

"How long does it take for the effects of one drink to wear off?" she asks. The Mets team says half an hour; the Yankees, two hours. Ayres tells them the right answer, one hour, and the boys groan.

"How quickly does alcohol reach the brain?" she asks. The Mets answer less than a minute, and gain two bases on the baseball diamond propped up against the blackboard at the front of the room. The boys do high-fives and slap each other on the back.

The game continues, covering questions on the effects of tobacco, alcohol, and drugs. The Yankees finally win, and

Ayres gives each team member a small Yankee pennant to take home. The boys make her promise to let them play again next time. She agrees, laughing, and puts the board away.

Ayres announces that she is taking the group to McDonald's in the Boys Club van to celebrate Derrick's tenth birthday. They jump up, eager to go. Elbert comes over and shyly hugs her, and asks if he can sit next to her at supper.

As they leave, Ayres says, "The boys get some drug prevention at school, but their classes are so big they don't pay attention very well and they don't get to practice the way we do here. The younger we can start the better— when they're still eager to learn. Kids grow up real fast out on those streets, and drugs are everywhere."

■

Since 1987 the Boys and Girls Clubs have been targeting very high-risk children in more than a hundred housing projects across the country. Recent evaluations report substantial reductions in cocaine and crack use, drug crime, and vandalism within the projects as well as improved school behavior and parental involvement.[8] Eric Goplerud, a prevention expert at the National Office of Drug Control Policy, believes the Boys and Girls Clubs fill a critical void: "Three million of the country's most vulnerable boys and girls live in housing projects. There are very few programs that offer them high-quality prevention teaching as well as challenging, supervised activities. The Boys and Girls Clubs' Smart Moves is a real catalyst for change for these very high-risk children, their families, and their communities."

The impact of drug prevention programs on other problems such as truancy, delinquency, and early pregnancy has not yet been tested. However, programs which reduce school failure and delinquency also report progress against alcohol and drug use. The Seattle Social Development Project (SSDP), begun in 1981 by Dr. David Hawkins at the University of Washington, is designed especially for children from high-crime neighborhoods. SSDP aims to reduce their risks for later problems by strengthening the bonds among children, families, and schools. Parents are taught to monitor, reward, and discipline their children, while teachers are trained to provide clear instructions, maintain order, and resolve conflicts. Children are taught to resist negative peer pressures and to work in cooperative learning groups in the classroom to master academic subjects.

Numerous evaluations over the past ten years report substantial improvement among SSDP participants, including fewer school expulsions, less delinquency, and reduced alcohol use. A study in 1991 of SSDP's impact on poor, inner-city children found that significantly fewer SSDP girls had begun smoking, drinking, or using drugs by the end of sixth grade than other girls. Although the program did not have a similar effect on boys, it did reduce their involvement in delinquency.[9]

Among those at greatest risk for substance abuse are the children of drug addicts. Strengthening Families is one of the few programs in the country which works directly with recovering drug addicts and their very young children. Developed by Dr. Karol Kumpfer at the University of Utah in Salt Lake City, Strengthening Families teaches parents how to improve communications with their children and to reduce conflict at home. At the same time, children learn social skills to reduce their vulnerability to alcohol and drugs.

Since 1986, Strengthening Families has been tested in over 500 families in Salt Lake City; Detroit; Denver; Selma, Alabama; Hawaii; and Iowa. Evaluations report that children who participate in the program have fewer problems, attend school more regularly, and use much less tobacco and alcohol. Since the children are very young—generally between the ages of five and ten—few have tried drugs, although many have begun experimenting with smoking and drinking.[10]

Though Strengthening Families changes children's attitudes toward tobacco and alcohol, it seems not to have the same effect on attitudes toward drugs. Dr. Kumpfer attributes this difference to family values: "These are children of drug addicts who might still be using drugs even though they are in treatment. The family culture tolerates drug use. The children may be afraid their parents will be angry if they say they intend not to use drugs—it may seem like a fundamental rejection of the family."

Since January 1991, the Safe Haven Program, which is based on Strengthening Families, has been working with recovering drug addicts and their children at Detroit's Salvation Army Harbor Light residential drug treatment center. "We're trying to teach parents how to bring more coherence into their family life," explains Dr. Susan Bridges, the program director. "They've been so busy with drugs they never took time with their kids. Now they're finding out how to really listen to their kids and even have fun with them. These kids have had to take on a lot of responsibility. We have to help them understand how to get the comfort and guidance they need. Within a month, you can see the progress; the children do better in school and the parents are more involved with them."

The grim economic circumstances facing these inner-city families have made treatment more difficult. Half the original group has dropped out since completing the three-month residential stay at Harbor Light, while the retention rate at other Strengthening Families programs is 75 percent. "Our clients drop out because they have major crises quite apart from drugs

—like homelessness, hunger, and no prospect of work. Detroit's social services cutbacks have left no safety net. We collect food and clothes for the children, but we can't find their parents homes and jobs," Dr. Bridges says.[11]

■

Five children, ranging in age from six to nine, meet two afternoons a week while their parents participate in a separate group. Marie S., a retired public school teacher who has had the Strengthening Families training, greets them affectionately. After the children quiet down, she gathers them around a small table. "How do you go about solving a problem at home if you're alone? What if your cat is gone?" she begins.

David R., a cherubic boy sitting next to her, answers, "You could call the cat, or go out and look for it."

"But what could happen if you go out?" Mrs. S. asks.

The children volunteer all at once: "You could get snatched by someone." "You could get hurt." "You could get lost." She urges them to take turns and praises them for thinking of all the things that might happen. She suggests that they might ask their neighbors for help, or wait for their parents or older brothers or sisters to come home.

"What do you do if someone offers you a beer or some weed?" Mrs. S. asks. Franklin G. waves his hand, jumping up from the table, "I would turn my back and walk away. Drinking could eat up your life."

The children practice saying no to drugs and alcohol, acting out both roles, laughing and nudging each other. After they have finished, Mrs. S. asks, "What do you do when you see an abandoned house?" Felicia J., her braids neatly tied with yellow ribbons, answers, "You should walk on by. There might be someone in there with guns."

Daniele H. interrupts, "I dreamed about something really scary last night, but I didn't want to tell my mom. I was afraid she'd get mad at me." Mrs. S. hugs her and says, "It's important to tell your mom how you feel. But if your parents don't want to hear, who else can you express your feelings to?" The children call out, "Your teacher, your grandmother, your older sister."

Marie S. asks them to get ready to go to the cafeteria to meet their parents for supper. On her way out, she explains, "The old definitions of family don't exist anymore for a lot of these kids. Their parents grew up in families of alcoholics and drug addicts, and now they're addicts, too. None of them has ever experienced stable, caring family relationships either as a parent or a child. We're trying to help the kids learn how to cope and find other resources when their parents let them down."

That evening, the parents' group has five mothers. Louise J., the group leader, asks them how they are doing with the contracts they worked out with their children to help the family function better. She reminds them, "It's important for your kids to know what you expect of them, just as you need to know what they expect from you."

"I've got my hands full with Felicia," a tall, slender woman says wearily. "She's very demanding and bosses the other kids around. Even though she agreed to our contract last week, now she refuses to clean up her room like she promised. Then I start hollering at her."

"Maybe you got to give her warnings and set limits and then stick to whatever the punishment is," another mother responds. "I've been trying that with David and it works real good."

"Sometimes if you don't discipline kids they think you don't care, like not putting them to bed at a certain time," explains Mrs. J. "Setting limits helps them learn self-control." She then turns to Felicia's mother, adding, "Maybe you need to go over the contract and let Felicia tell you why she is having problems following it. Changing the contract doesn't mean you've failed. Maybe she's too young to handle some of the things you're asking. You should talk it through when we meet with the kids later."

Have the women all taken time, Mrs. J. asks, to discuss their feelings with their children? Have they encouraged the children to talk about their feelings? One mother answers, "Daniele doesn't want to talk. She just smiles and goes on playing."

"Daniele might be scared to express negative feelings because she doesn't know how you will react," Mrs. J. suggests. "What about praise? Remember how important it is to tell your kids about the good things they do."

"Is there such a thing as making up for lost praise?" Daniele's mother asks. "I've been thinking about something good she did a couple of weeks ago, and I didn't say anything. Can I go back now and do it?"

Franklin's mother throws back her head, laughing. "Sure you can, girl. That's what our lives are all about—going back and getting it right this time."

■

High-risk children need special help breaking through the denial surrounding drug and alcohol problems, whether they live in inner-city Detroit or affluent Westchester County. Strengthening Families, like Project Healthy Choices, helps very young children find the words to describe the destructive reality of substance abuse in their daily lives and gives them support in dealing with it.

The most promising prevention programs respond to the way

children think at different stages in their development. Bank Street's Eileen Wasow explains, "Young kids need to play with ideas in order to integrate their knowledge into a workable framework. They want to try things out, like being the bad guy and then the good guy. They need to talk about the real questions in their lives, like, Would my brother use a gun if drug dealers come? If my mother is high on crack, who do I ask for help? How do I feel secure? They need to have adult permission to come to terms in their own way with their daily experience. Then they can learn refusal skills and other ways of reshaping their reality."

We know that prevention programs for high-risk children should begin as early as possible, long before they experiment with tobacco and alcohol. As the Seattle Social Development Project suggests, efforts to reduce early school failure—a key predictor for later problems—may also hold promise against substance abuse. Children who have participated in preschool enrichment programs such as Head Start perform better and stay in school longer. In later years, they are more likely to be employed and less likely to be arrested than those who have not participated in these programs.[12]

Head Start currently reaches fewer than half of the nation's 2 million preschool-age children growing up in poverty. In 1994, Congress authorized Head Start for another four years with legislation designed to extend coverage to all eligible three-, four-, and five-year-olds, as well as to very young children through a "zero-to-three" initiative. Despite the legislative commitment Congress has made to the program, it is unlikely that they will approve the funds necessary to achieve Head Start's goals. Although President Clinton recommended increasing the program's $3.3 billion budget to $4.05 billion for 1995, at this writing the Congress has only approved an additional $210 million. Fully funding the Head Start program would be an important step in making poor children less vulnerable not only to school dropout and delinquency but also to substance abuse.

We know that family and community attitudes are vital in building a child's resistance to tobacco, alcohol, and drugs. For very high-risk children with little real connection to their families and schools, there has to be at least one haven where they can find counseling and support. Programs like the Boys and Girls Clubs which link prevention with recreational, educational, and vocational opportunities improve the chances that children will be able to resist pressures to use and sell drugs.

Taking LST to homeless shelters, Smart Moves to housing projects, and Student Assistance Programs to foster-care facilities engages children who would otherwise not be reached by prevention programs. The highest-risk children and their families are often the hardest to retain because their lives are disrupted by drug addiction and poverty. But as Strengthening Families shows, those who participate can make substantial progress despite these difficulties. Concentrating prevention resources on the most vulnerable boys and girls reduces the likelihood of continuing cycles of addiction and family disintegration. Without such help, generations of children will be lost to drugs, crime, and despair.

5

.

Dealing
with Dealers

Street drug markets have spread across the country, bringing with them crime, violence, and death. In a 1994 survey, police departments in the nation's fifteen largest cities reported 1,500 drug markets, ranging from half a dozen in Indianapolis to over three hundred each in New York City and Chicago. Street markets also operate in smaller cities, such as Pasadena and Des Moines.[1]

Although street markets had been flourishing in many areas since the 1960s, the surge in cocaine's popularity in the 1980s generated enormous new demand. Crack further expanded street dealing, attracting buyers who could not afford cocaine, which in 1988 sold for $100 a gram. Crack was available in much cheaper units and produced even more intense highs. Crack can also be easily manufactured from cocaine and then resold for three times its original cost. Thousands of people who had not been dealers before jumped at this new entrepreneurial opportunity. Crack transformed the economics of street dealing by guaranteeing large profits with minimal investment, even for low-level sellers.[2]

Street drug markets attract "drive-through" buyers from wealthier neighborhoods, particularly the suburbs. Deals are completed in a matter of seconds with little personal contact. Particular street markets often offer particular drugs. In Washington, D.C., a police officer explained, "If you want marijuana, you go to Fifteenth and Girard. Coke is over at Florida and Sherman. If you're a yuppie suburbanite, you cruise over to Twelfth and O Street and pick up one of the kids standing there and he'll take you to where you can get what you want."

In Pilgrim Village, one of Detroit's poorer neighborhoods, dealers installed outside chutes on the side of a house so customers could exchange cash for drugs without getting out of their cars. "We called it the Burger King," recalls Charlene Johnson, who directs REACH (Reach Everyone Administer Care and Help), a grass-roots community group in Pilgrim Village. "People drove by day and night placing their orders through the speaker box, picking up their drugs, and taking off."

Street markets also spill over into more affluent areas, like New York City's Washington Square Park near New York University, where dealers drove out students, young families, and elderly residents during much of the 1980s. The fear of violence is common in many communities. T. Willard Fair, president of the Urban League of Miami, says, "Our kids are being forced to play inside because they're afraid of being shot in their own front yards. They can't go to the parks or playgrounds, they can't even go to school without being threatened. We are all hostages in this drug war."

In many neighborhoods, crack houses flourish where people

go to buy and use drugs as well as sell or trade sex for drugs. Some crack houses are upscale, like the Harlem brownstone which Lillian G., now a recovering addict at New York City's Phoenix House, ran with her husband for six years. "We had nice cafe tables, candles, music, a fully stocked bar, and quality drugs," she recalls. "The rooms upstairs which customers could rent by the hour were kept up really well, clean sheets each time. We had regular clients, mostly from outside Harlem, and they spent a lot of money at our place. We paid two guys to guard the door and make sure fights didn't break out. We never had any trouble with the cops."

But most crack houses are semiabandoned, dilapidated buildings, where strung out, often violent customers come and go all night long, littering the neighborhood with crack vials, used needles, and guns, sad vestiges of the drug epidemic. Spike Lee's 1991 movie *Jungle Fever* vividly portrays the "Taj Mahal" of crack houses, a cavernous, ruined warehouse in Harlem filled with hundreds of crack addicts huddled on old mattresses, the glow of their crack pipes the only light in the gloomy, smoke-filled interior.

In many deteriorating inner-city blocks, property values have dropped sharply. Owners who cannot sell their buildings decide either to rent to anyone, including drug dealers, or to abandon their property. The crack epidemic has accelerated this flight from the inner city, leaving behind very few role models for children growing up there.

Living in neighborhoods where illegal drugs are bought and sold openly greatly increases the risks to children. Dealers, with their ready cash and flashy clothes and cars, become powerful role models for youngsters eager to imitate successful adults. If dealers are allowed to operate openly, children also perceive a level of community apathy, if not outright toleration, toward drugs.

Dr. Susan Bridges, the director of Detroit's Safe Haven program, observes, "It should be no surprise that sixty percent of the kids in this city drop out of school—and for girls it's closer to eighty percent. The role models they see growing up in many of these neighborhoods are drug dealers and prostitutes. A lot of their mothers are on crack, and they never see their fathers. They've never been inside a church, which used to hold the black community together. These kids feel totally hopeless."

Dealing also offers powerful economic incentives, especially in low-income communities. For many people who have limited employment opportunities, drug dealing—which generates $49 billion in annual sales nationwide—provides a substantial source of income.[3] A 1990 Rand Corporation study confirmed this. Washington, D.C., street dealers who work about four hours a day reported earning $2,000 a month on average.[4] Two-thirds also hold regular jobs paying about $800 a month. For them, dealing is a kind of lucrative "moonlighting," which supplements their legitimate salaries with untaxed, illegal income.

These are not the high-stakes returns associated in the public mind with drug dealing, certainly not enough to buy flashy foreign cars and suburban villas. But within the economy of the inner city where many dealers have low overhead and can live with family or friends, a tax-free income of $24,000 a year (to use the Rand figures) can buy a good deal of luxury—clothes, jewelry, electronic equipment—and provide some help for the dealers' impoverished families. Many street dealers also use cocaine and heroin daily, and spend at least a quarter of their income on their own drug habit.

Inner-city children have also been recruited into the crack trade, working for dealers as lookouts and couriers, as well as handling smaller sales. One-sixth of the ninth- and tenth-graders included in the Rand study sold drugs. But less than a third of them used drugs, compared to 95 percent of the adult dealers. These youngsters often find the allure of high earnings irresistible, despite the risks involved.

A taxi driver on Chicago's South Side shares the lament of many parents: "If you locked up every kid on every corner, there'd be more kids [on the corners] in an hour. They're not willing to work for minimum wage at McDonald's when they can make hundreds of dollars working for the dealers. My own son got caught up in dealing, even though we're a solid work-ing-class family. One of his best friends in high school became a famous jockey, on the cover of *Ebony*, and his other friend became a big drug dealer. Billy wanted to be up there, too. He needed to be a big success and thought that was the only way to do it."

In private drug markets, where buyers are referred to sellers by friends, deals are done in offices, clubs, or homes. Much like white-collar crime, these transactions are usually well hidden from public view. Street drug markets, however, are highly visible, operating in inner-city neighborhoods where the concentration of police officers is generally much lower than in affluent areas.

Miami's T. Willard Fair sees drug dealing as a particular problem for the black community. "This is the most formidable foe we've faced since slavery. Someone is selling death to us, and we're letting it happen. The only reason drugs are sold on the streets of my community and not in the fancy suburbs is that we accept dealing as a legitimate business," he explains. "My community is the white man's market for purchasing drugs, where he goes to stock up for his weekend parties. I can't count the number of people who benefit from this traffic—kids get toys at Christmas, turkeys at Thanksgiving; families rely on the income. But we're being poisoned because we're being rewarded for irresponsibility."

The cash flow generated by street drug markets does little to strengthen the underlying economy of poor neighborhoods. Most profits vanish quickly into consumer goods and luxury items rather than legitimate business investments which would create steady employment for local residents. And dealers face substantial risks—arrest, imprisonment, injury, and addiction —damaging their prospects for long careers.

■

Some neighborhoods are fighting back, driving out dealers and reclaiming their streets. They are reducing crime, violence, and fear, and restoring a sense of community and shared hope. Behind each inspired block leader who has taken the lead in combating street dealing, there is a single, crystallizing moment when anger and determination become a decision to act.

For Doris Watkins, a community organizer for the Marshall Heights Community Development Organization in Washington, D.C., the death of a neighbor spurred her to action. "I had been living in this neighborhood for five years in a real nice little house I was fixing up for me and my baby girl. Crack came and we had dealers on every corner. Cars driving by all night, gunshots so you couldn't sleep, and we were scared to death," Watkins remembers. "One evening, the woman across the street was sitting on her porch with her husband and seven-year-old son. She got shot by a stray bullet and died right there in front of our eyes. That was the turning point. I said, 'Now's the time. We can't sit here and take this any longer.' "

In 1989 Watkins organized citizen patrols, recruiting residents to cover a five-block radius in their neighborhoods each night. The patrols wear bright orange shirts and hats and are armed with walkie-talkies, cameras, and notepads.

"We jot down car tag numbers and descriptions of people who drive up to the dealers, and we keep in touch with each other about what's going on," Watkins explains. "We take pictures, too, sometimes without any film in the cameras. The important thing is to let them know we're watching them and reporting to the police. Diplomats don't want their tags recorded and passed along to the police. And a husband who lives in Arlington sure doesn't want his wife to know he's coming over here to buy drugs."

Watkins's neighborhood now has five patrols which work from 7:00 to 10:00 P.M. seven days a week. Sometimes the dealers harass them, shouting and calling them names, occasionally shooting pellet guns over their heads. The patrols call in police support whenever necessary, and so far no one has been injured.

The police have responded by stepping up their regular patrols of the area. Open street dealing has declined dramatically. "Dealers can't stand the hassle of having us around, so they move on somewhere else, or do their business inside," Watkins says. "But we have to keep focusing on the area or they'll come right back."

A recent survey of antidrug efforts in seventeen major cities found that only seven had citizen patrols, despite their demonstrated effectiveness in reducing street dealing.[5] Recruitment is the major obstacle. Doris Watkins, like other community organizers, knows that it is easier to mobilize neighborhoods where some people own their homes, giving them a greater stake in its future, than in areas where most residents are renters. She points out East Gate, a public housing project a mile from her house, with rubble and trash blowing against its high surrounding fence. "I haven't been able to get one single group to patrol in there," Watkins says. "A police officer is assigned to the project twenty-four hours a day, but they can cover only one space. Unless you get residents involved, you have a hopeless case. So I'm trying a new approach. I've gotten a couple of people from the project to help us plant a big garden across the street, and we call it the East Gate Garden Club. I can't get them to patrol, but I can get them to put seeds in the ground. At least we can work together on that. Maybe they'll begin to get a sense of ownership in what's going on in their neighborhood."

In many cities, anticrack rallies have drawn media attention to drug dealing and have helped persuade residents to take action. In Detroit's Pilgrim Village, REACH has used marches to publicize community opposition to drugs. On October 31, 1988, REACH organized a Halloween funeral procession across town to Detroit police headquarters, led by a hearse, to "bury" crack. For three days, REACH declared Pilgrim Village a drug-free zone; residents marched through the streets from 6:00 P.M. until midnight. "We knew we had to make a big, visual protest against crack that would get people's attention, and give them courage to fight back," recalls Charlene Johnson. "The police were very supportive and marched with us. We formed a group to continue the antidrug patrols and work with the police. We do monthly marches, which get good media coverage. Last Easter, we crucified crack and crime on Good Friday."

Although citizen patrols can have a powerful effect in reducing flagrant drug dealing, reclaiming neighborhoods like Pilgrim Village requires much more. REACH began in 1982 as the community ministry of the Reverend Lee Earl, pastor of Detroit's Twelfth Street Baptist Church. It promotes community involvement by engaging residents in a variety of volunteer programs: distributing food to elderly residents in exchange for a small donation; operating a day-care center in the church basement for forty local children; and running a summer program offering teenagers field trips, sports, and camping.

The heart of REACH's effort is buying and renovating dilapidated houses and then selling them to neighborhood residents. "Drug deals were going on all day long in a house across from our church," Charlene Johnson recalls. "We realized we had to control our environment by ownership. We persuaded the elderly owner of the house, who hadn't lived in the neighborhood for years, to evict the tenants and sell the house to the church. We renovated it with volunteers, and in 1983 a single mother and her two children rented the house from the church. Once people saw what could be done, they started getting involved."

Johnson's husband, a carpenter, trained her and other residents in building skills; she is now a licensed contractor in charge of REACH's renovation program. Since then, REACH has bought and renovated two dozen houses, largely with volunteer labor. In 1990 REACH opened Mrs. Funderburg's Heart and Soul Cafeteria on Pilgrim Avenue, the main traffic artery through northwest Detroit, to provide jobs as well as healthy meals for area residents. Again REACH relied on volunteer labor and local minority tradespeople to convert the large abandoned building into a restaurant.

Open drug dealing has virtually disappeared from the streets of Pilgrim Village. From 1985 to 1990, violent crimes declined by about 10 percent and property crimes by 25 percent.[6] Johnson believes that REACH's programs can best combat drug abuse and crime by changing the quality of people's lives. "There are so many forces in the black community that destroy our self-esteem. We have to provide real work, real responsibility so that people can be successful," she says. "Everyone who works with us sees that there is hope. We don't have to depend on outsiders to make it happen for us."

Other communities have begun "reclamation" through massive clean-up projects, removing tons of trash which accumulate around abandoned houses and in vacant lots. Then they move on to close down local crack houses. In 1989 Miami's Urban League launched Operation POP (Push Out the Pusher) in predominantly black Liberty City. "We cleaned up two hundred lots and the pushers kept running our people off, so the police had to come in and protect us," T. Willard Fair recalls. "Then we tore down our first crack house, after getting a court order condemning it. Since then, we've torn down three hundred more." The Urban League set up a tracking system to prevent tenants who had been evicted for drug sales from renting again in the neighborhood. "We must go after the pusher with a zeal that is unbelievable and make drugs the most undesirable thing you can do in our community. We're sending a message that drug pushers don't have a place to lay their heads," Fair declares.

Community efforts to rid the streets of drug dealers often can change the way people view law enforcement. Inner-city residents who have seen the police as adversaries now learn to work with them in fighting dealers, the common enemy. "Someone fooled us into thinking white policemen were worse than black criminals," Fair observes, "but crack blew that crazy notion right out of the water. We need law enforcement on our side."

Indeed, residents in many poor communities have often felt victimized by the police. Before REACH began organizing Detroit's Pilgrim Village, police called it "the Hole" and reportedly refused to answer calls there. To get police patrols into her southeast Washington neighborhood, Doris Watkins persuaded residents to demonstrate at the local precinct. "The police had no respect for us, and refused to help us," she recalls. "But when they saw we meant business, they finally responded. Now we have regular patrols on our streets, and our 'grannies group' —seven women in their late sixties who walk the kids home from the school bus stop every afternoon to make sure the dealers won't hassle them—even has an undercover cop who drives by to keep an eye on them."

Many communities have also begun working with government agencies for the first time, giving them a sense of the larger political possibilities for effecting change. Audrey Brantley, head of the W. D. Edson Neighborhood Improvement Association in the poor northwest section of Pasadena, California, spends much of her time learning "how the system works so we can use it to benefit our neighborhood."

In 1990 Brantley and her neighbors persuaded the local state assembly representative to sponsor a law holding landlords responsible for drug dealing on their properties. The police have followed up, pinpointing buildings which generate the most frequent calls.

"What we are doing is sending a clear message to landlords that they have to pay attention to what kind of tenants they rent to," Brantley explains. "And it's working—a lot of owners have kicked out dealers rather than have their property seized."

Code enforcement is a powerful weapon which community organizers across the country are using against dealers. Crack houses can often be condemned because of housing-code violations or failure to have certificates of occupancy, required fire-safety systems, and emergency exits. Many single-family houses have been illegally converted into unlicensed rooming houses where drugs are used and sold. Using civil codes to go after properties where dealers operate can help deprive them of a base in the neighborhood.

"A key part of our job is to get city agencies to give our neighborhood the same kind of attention they give more affluent areas," Miami's T. Willard Fair explains. "The tools are there, and we're finally beginning to use them."

Police departments are becoming more innovative as well, devising new strategies to break up street markets. In Houston and Indianapolis, police have set up blockades on the periphery of the drug market area where they check drivers' licenses, registration, and insurance on incoming automobiles. Area residents are given special identifications to allow them to come and go freely; prospective drug buyers often turn away rather than identify themselves. In Kansas City, Fort Lauderdale, and Yakima, Washington, police mail postcards to owners of cars seen cruising near drug markets, warning that their vehicle was observed in an area known to be frequented by drug dealers and prostitutes. Citizen and police patrols record the license plate numbers of these cars, and owners are traced through the Department of Motor Vehicles. These warnings sharply reduce drive-through traffic since many customers fear that their families or employers will find out about their activities.

In Inkster, Michigan, a working-class suburb of Detroit, drive-through crack markets flourished in several housing projects in the late 1980s. Police first set up checkpoints to discourage buyers, which drove some away. The police then began seizing cars in which drugs were found, and charging owners $750 to get them back. The drive-through market rapidly disappeared.

Mark A. R. Kleiman, a drug policy expert at Harvard University's John F. Kennedy School of Government, points out that "low-arrest strategies can break up street markets without swamping courts and jails with cases and prisoners they can't possibly handle. They combine high deterrence with low cost, by making punishment immediate and certain without making it drastic or expensive. It's a good way to get the most bang for the enforcement buck."

High-arrest strategies like "street sweeps" remain popular because they demonstrate dramatic action against drug crime. Neighborhood residents are generally relieved to have drug markets disabled even temporarily. However, without sustained community involvement, enforcement campaigns which generate large numbers of arrests rarely have a lasting effect.

The New York City Police Department targeted street markets on Manhattan's Lower East Side in Operation Pressure Point, begun in 1983. During the first year, burglaries fell by more than one-third, robberies dropped by half, and homicides by almost two-thirds. At the same time, some parts of the neighborhood became "gentrified" as affluent professionals moved in, renovating buildings and reclaiming the area. After the concentrated police presence of Operation Pressure Point diminished in 1987, the street markets did not return in the "gentrified" areas in large part because the neighborhood itself had improved with the active involvement of its residents. But in unimproved areas, street markets reappeared.[7]

In March 1988 the New York City Police Department tried a new approach to intensive street enforcement, using mobile Tactical Narcotics Teams (TNT) to carry out "buy and bust" patrols within a narrowly targeted area for a ninety-day period. In 1992 TNT was responsible for one-fifth of the city's 65,000 drug arrests. In Southeast Queens, the first TNT operation substantially reduced drug dealing, but after the special police unit withdrew, dealing resumed. High-intensity police activity in a few particular neighborhoods generally cannot be sustained permanently because those resources are also in great demand in other areas of the city. In addition, the huge numbers of arrests generated by street sweeps usually inundate the criminal justice system, clogging the courts and jails, so that eventually the police are required to move to alternative approaches.[8]

■

One enforcement strategy which promises to have longer-term impact on street drug markets is community policing, where patrol officers are assigned to work closely with neighborhood residents to solve recurring crime problems. In New York City's Community Patrol Officer Program (CPOP), specially trained officers work with local groups to bring pressure on drug dealers.

In contrast with intensive, short-term enforcement efforts like TNT, community policing relies on continuing neighborhood vigilance to prevent drug dealers from returning.

In some cities, police officers are leaving their squad cars to patrol on foot or bicycle, establishing a visible, reassuring presence which also disrupts dealing. Police trailers serve as local command posts within besieged neighborhoods, warning dealers away and providing a focal point for contact with community groups. In addition, officers work to improve conditions in the neighborhood by seeking better services from city agencies. Cutting back the underbrush in a local park, clearing trash from open spaces, and increasing street lighting can make an area much less attractive to dealers. City agencies are more likely to respond quickly to police requests than to residents of poor neighborhoods who seek these services unassisted.

Linking law enforcement to the community gives residents the support they need to take control of their streets. Michael Clark, president of the Citizens Committee of New York, which helps organize neighborhoods to drive out dealers, believes that "street sweeps cannot be the first and only technique, which they are in many cities. We have to get away from the body-count mentality that has dominated drug enforcement for the past decade. Real progress should not be measured by the numbers of arrests but by lasting improvement in the quality of life in besieged neighborhoods."

In Pasadena, twenty-five of the Police Department's 220 officers are assigned full-time to the Neighborhood Crime Task Force which concentrates on open drug dealing and street crime. Task Force officers work with Audrey Brantley's Neighborhood Association, selecting block captains to organize watch groups, to pursue negligent landlords, and to drive dealers out of local apartment buildings.

"I couldn't send my grandkids to the park across the street

because the dealers would be hanging around hassling them," Brantley recalls. "But we were able to work with the police to get rid of them, and we got the Parks Department to fix it up again, and now we all go there."

Police know many residents by name, assist in emergency situations such as driving a sick child to the hospital, and take part in neighborhood events, such as an annual picnic which raises money for the Neighborhood Association's beautification efforts. Between 1988 and 1992, drug crime in Pasadena declined by 40 percent, and assaults on police officers dropped by 30 percent.[9]

■

While law enforcement alone is not sufficient to eliminate drug markets, it can measurably increase the risks for dealers and buyers even without arresting them. Seizing automobiles discourages suburban drive-through customers in many cities—and because seizure proceedings are civil rather than criminal, a lesser standard of proof is required. The practical effect is that cars may be legally seized without a formal arrest, punishing buyers without placing additional strains on the criminal justice system.

Half the cars seized in New York City from 1991 to 1993 belonged to suburbanites who said they did not believe they had serious drug problems. Almost all had been able to hide their drug use from families, friends, and employers, and never anticipated being caught. Sterling Johnson, a federal district court judge who was special narcotics prosecutor for New York City from 1973 to 1991, says, "When one of these kids comes home without Daddy's car, the criminal justice system is often the least of his worries. It shakes up the whole family and forces them to recognize there's a problem they need to get to work on changing."[10]

The presence of police officers in neighborhoods where drug markets flourish increases the "hassle" factor that dealers and customers must face. Making the drug business more inconvenient can bring about immediate disruptions in street markets. Faced with losing their customers and the possibility of arrest, dealers often move to safer areas, and prospective buyers have to make greater efforts to find new connections. Increasing the "search time" for buyers can reduce their drug use, even if drug prices remain unchanged. This is an especially important deterrent for people who are still experimenting with drugs but not yet using them regularly.

Breaking up street markets is one of the most promising strategies for reducing crime and drug addiction. "The traditional goal of drug enforcement is to drive up drug prices," explains Harvard's Mark A. R. Kleiman. "Higher prices tend to reduce drug abuse but they also lead some drug users to steal more to support their habits. Pushing the 'search time' up for buyers by disrupting street markets actually reduces property crime as well as drug use, because drug users who can't find dealers end up spending less money on drugs. This makes neighborhoods safer and also may encourage addicts to find treatment."

■

Even with the encouraging results coming out of these newer approaches, police officials are not deluded about the ability of law enforcement to combat drug abuse. "For too long, we have expected law enforcement to eliminate the nation's drug problem," observes Frances Mullen, former administrator of the U.S. Drug Enforcement Administration and deputy director of the FBI. "While it obviously has an important role to play, we won't have any lasting success until we start working on reducing the huge demand for drugs."

The immense popularity of DARE, the elementary school prevention program taught by police officers, reflects this changing perception of law enforcement. Although DARE has not been found to reduce tobacco, alcohol, or drug use, the program does improve the way children view the police. Police officer Susan Glaser, who teaches prevention to fifth-graders in San Francisco, comments, "In the schools where I teach, I see kids who are already predisposed to getting in trouble. They have numerous contacts with police at home and on the street. But in my classes, they see that cops have a more human side, that we care about helping them stay away from crime and drugs."

DARE also increases the involvement of police departments in the community. Dr. Richard Clayton, director of the Center for Prevention Research at the University of Kentucky, who has conducted several evaluations of DARE, points out that "DARE connects traditional law enforcement officials to the children they teach in school, their families, and the neighborhood. That kind of connection is the essence of effective community policing."

Reshaping traditional definitions of law enforcement's role changes the way police officials view drug addicts as well. When police officers engage in community efforts to improve neighborhoods or teach prevention to schoolchildren, they learn more about the causes of addiction and they are less likely to consider addicts simply as criminals. Benjamin Ward, New York City's police commissioner from 1984 to 1989, believes that "crack is a social ailment which is not going to be solved with cops, courts, and prisons." Bruce Philpott, the former police chief of Pasadena, thinks that value judgments about addiction get in the way of effective police work. "I don't declare we're going to shoot every drug user, like some chiefs do," Philpott says. "That communicates to officers that these people are worthless. We are not their enemies. Law enforcement is part of the consequence if you choose to use or sell drugs, and we help them recognize they've reached bottom. We have an opportunity to turn people's lives around if they respect us and see us as an arm of the community."

Most street dealers are also addicts. The threat of arrest and imprisonment has not proved an effective deterrent for people desperate to finance their next fix. Making treatment readily available makes better sense, particularly within the criminal justice system, where many street dealers spend at least part of their lives.

■

When dealers invade a neighborhood, they become powerful role models, showing children that selling drugs, not hard work, is the route to riches. Community efforts to drive out dealers immediately change that perception. As the middle-class market for cocaine shrinks, street dealing will offer fewer opportunities for fast profits. Competition for remaining buyers may lead to increased violence among dealers, particularly those who are themselves addicts. As dealing becomes more risky and less lucrative, it will lose some of its attraction to inner-city youngsters. But they will also require real alternatives, including solid educational, employment, and recreational opportunities.[11]

Grass-roots groups such as REACH are trying to create these alternatives in their own neighborhoods. Other local groups are beginning to connect to citywide prevention efforts. In Washington, D.C., children from Doris Watkins's Marshall Heights neighborhood now participate in STAR prevention classes at school, a major initiative of the Corporation Against Drug Abuse (CADA), an antidrug coalition established in 1988 by local business leaders. Connie Bush, director of

CADA's Community Prevention Program, explains, "If we want to protect our kids, this is the place to begin. First we have to get rid of the dealers and then we have to make sure our kids get the best prevention teaching available so they know how to resist drugs."

In neighborhoods like Pilgrim Village, Liberty City, and northwest Pasadena, citizen efforts to drive out drug dealing often depend on a few highly committed men and women who work around the clock to sustain neighborhood participation. "Apathy is our greatest enemy," says Audrey Brantley about her Neighborhood Association. "It's a constant fight against the dealers. They're like weeds, they pop out everywhere. To get the whole neighborhood involved is very tough. I've got a hardworking small group and I have to pull the rest in by their hair."

As Audrey Brantley and other community organizers have learned, succeeding over the long run takes more than creating citizen patrols. Neighborhood residents must learn how to get help from police and city agencies and to work with them in a way that is truly collaborative. Without strong outside support, neighborhood efforts run the risk of exhausting themselves.

Street drug dealing is one of the most flagrant symptoms of the poverty, racism, and despair that are corroding many cities. Despite daily threats of violence, courageous individuals across the country have taken on drug dealers in order to make a better life for themselves and their children. Their hard-won victories are often brief as dealers fight to regain their territory. Unless citizen efforts receive support from the larger community and new resources for their neighborhoods, lasting progress will not be possible.

6
∎

Driving Drugs from the Workplace

On August 28, 1991, a speeding New York City subway train jumped the rails and crashed into a tunnel wall, killing 5 people and injuring 170 others. A crack vial was found in the driver's cab, and the motorman himself (who had fled the scene) was drunk when he was apprehended four hours later.

The crash was a grim reminder of the dangers of drug and alcohol use on the job. Although there is no evidence that the motorman used crack that day, many people wondered how his drinking problem could have gone undetected. Until then, the public did not realize that the safety net had some awfully large holes. The New York City Transit Authority had periodically tested its employees for drug use since 1983, but it had never conducted unannounced, random testing. The U.S. Department of Transportation made random drug testing mandatory for mass transit workers in 1988, but court challenges by transport workers' unions across the country succeeded in suspending and then invalidating this requirement. In any case, formal alcohol testing had never been required; detection depended instead on what one senior union official called "the sharp eyes of the supervisor on duty and his sense of smell."[1]

The subway accident transformed policy overnight. The New York City Transit Authority initiated—with strong union support—random drug and alcohol testing for subway crews and bus drivers. And in Washington, D.C., the Department of Transportation mandated alcohol testing beginning in late 1992 for all transportation workers in safety-sensitive positions.

An earlier tragedy had already aroused public fears about drug use on the job. In January 1987, an Amtrak train crashed outside Baltimore, Maryland, killing sixteen holiday passengers. The train's engineer and brakeman had been smoking marijuana. Whatever ambivalence many Americans may have had about private drug use vanished in the train's wreckage. Powerful advertising by the Partnership for a Drug Free America highlighted the need to get drugs out of the workplace. Television spots, like one showing a school bus driver sniffing cocaine on her way to work, echoed our worst fears: even if we can prevent our children from trying drugs, we may not be able to protect them from injury or death caused by a substance abuser.

Yet despite this shift in attitudes, drug and alcohol use in the workforce remains widespread. Two-thirds of all adults who used illegal drugs at least once a month in 1992 were employed, a total of about 6.7 million people.[2] The National Institute of Drug Abuse (NIDA) estimates that 10 percent of the workforce is drug addicted or alcoholic. Illegal drug use varies by industry, ranging from 13 percent in transportation and 14 percent in retail to 22 percent in construction. Almost half of all employees with alcoholism problems are in professional fields, less than a third are manual laborers, and the rest are white-collar workers.[3]

The costs of drug use in the workplace—including lost productivity, absenteeism, accidents, medical claims, and thefts —amount to $60 billion a year. If alcohol is included, the annual total jumps to $140 billion. A 1991 study by the U.S. Postal Service found that workers whose pre-employment drug tests were positive (but who were hired anyway as part of the study) were 50 percent more likely to be fired, injured, disciplined, or absent than those who were drug-free. The U.S. Chamber of Commerce also found that employees who use drugs are one-third less productive and three times more likely to injure themselves or another person at work.[4]

The far-reaching cocaine epidemic forced business leaders to take a hard look at employee drug use. By the mid-1980s, they began to develop strategies to get drugs out of the workplace. At the same time, President Reagan made "user accountability" a major focus of his antidrug strategy. In 1986 he ordered all federal agencies to establish drug policies and to create employee assistance programs for workers with drug problems. Two years later, Congress passed the Drug Free Workplace Act, which requires all companies receiving federal contracts larger than $25,000 to establish antidrug policies and programs. By 1993 more than 80 percent of the nation's largest businesses (those with 250 employees or more) had done so.[5]

Although government leadership has encouraged the growth of drug-free workplace programs, businesses themselves have strong economic motives for reducing employee drug use. Thomas Van Etten, vice president of Sun Bank in Miami, believes that businesses cannot ignore drug use if they want to remain competitive. "Given the baby-boom bust, we're no longer going to be able to pick and choose among large pools of good applicants," Van Etten explains. "Increasingly we have to work with what we have, which means improving the quality and productivity of our workforce. Otherwise, we'll go out of business. Whether people want to recognize it or not, drugs have become a bottom-line issue."

Despite the proliferation of drug-free workplace programs, denial is still widespread. According to a 1990 survey, 90 percent of the CEOs of Fortune 500 companies believed drugs were a problem for American business, but only 27 percent thought drugs were a problem in their own companies.[6] As with drug abusers who resist seeking treatment, the greatest obstacle to developing effective drug policies in the workplace is often the view that drug abuse is someone else's problem.

At Capital Cities/ABC, the death of an employee from cocaine overdose in 1984 abruptly ended what Charles Keller, vice president for health, calls "the dream world we lived in where we thought our organization wouldn't have drug problems like the rest of society." President Dan Burke immediately set up a special working group, drawn from all of the company's divisions, to look into the problem. They found that the high-pressure, high-pay media business was a perfect match to the drug abuser profile, particularly for cocaine. More than one in four of their employees reported having used illegal drugs on the job.

"We had to attack the problem aggressively," recalls Keller. "We don't want anyone working here who uses drugs, even if that means we lose some creative people."

By 1985, Capital Cities had a tough new policy forbidding any illegal drug use. It also launched an antidrug poster campaign for its employees nationwide, and set up a toll-free twenty-four-hour-a-day hotline called "800-FIGHT-IT" to advise employees about drug treatment.

"By announcing that if you want to come to work you can't use, we're taking an important stand against this problem,"

Keller says. "People fear the loss of their jobs, which gives them a big incentive to get treatment if they need it. The workplace is the 'hot button' for change."

■

Most of the country's large companies have established employee assistance programs (EAPs) to help employees with drug and alcohol problems. In 1991, over 30 million American workers were covered by EAPs, compared to only 8 million in 1984. Some companies, like Wells Fargo Bank and Southern California Edison, have their own fully staffed in-house programs which provide counseling and treatment, but most businesses purchase these services from major providers like Aetna Life Insurance and Personnel and Performance Consultants, a St. Louis company.

By providing confidential assistance with substance abuse and other personal problems, EAPs have helped companies retain employees and reduce costs. Dr. Glen Houghie, vice president for health at IBM, reflects the thinking of many corporate executives: "We have a strong commitment to our employees to help them overcome their problems. It's a fair way of dealing with them but it also makes good business sense. We invest a lot of money in hiring and training—replacing an employee costs somewhere around fifty thousand dollars." In a three-year study of the financial impact of its EAP, the McDonnell Douglas Corporation reported a savings of $5.1 million from reduced medical claims, absenteeism, and turnover rates.

Some companies provide incentives to employees to use the EAP before their problems get out of control. "If we can prevent a catastrophe, we save time, money, and our employees' careers," says Sun Bank's Van Etten. Tropicana Orange Juice reimburses half the employee's insurance deductible if they stay off drugs for two years and the remaining half after three years.

Employees who resume drug use are fired. Since the program's inception in 1989, 80 percent of those who have sought help are still drug-free and working for the company.

"This is a business deal," explains Martin Gutfreund, Tropicana's vice president for government affairs. "We say to our employees, We will invest in you to the extent you invest in yourselves, but it's completely up to you."

Capital Cities/ABC pays half the insurance deductible for employees who complete treatment through the 800-FIGHT-IT service. "We shaped an EAP to meet the needs of our company so that treatment is very accessible through pre-selected programs all over the country," Charles Keller explains. "One of our local TV anchormen, for example, had a drug problem but didn't want to go off the air for a month to go into residential treatment. So the program arranged for him to go into the station to do his show every day and then come back in—a little like work release."

■

Highly accurate tests are now available to determine the presence of drug metabolites in urine. Marijuana can be detected for several weeks, particularly if use is heavy and frequent, but cocaine and amphetamines are difficult to trace for more than forty-eight hours. Heroin and other opiates can be identified two to four days after use. However, despite the reliability of the technology, negligent laboratory work can still produce inaccurate results. The U.S. Navy had to reverse all positive findings for certain drug tests in 1981, and rehire the people fired as a result of sloppy lab work. In 1990 a federal court ordered the New York City Transit Authority to compensate and rehire hundreds of workers who had been fired because of faulty marijuana tests conducted from 1984 to 1987.

Federal guidelines adopted in 1988 require certification of

drug-testing facilities by NIDA and impose tough quality standards and frequent inspections of laboratories. Nonetheless, in 1991 NIDA reported finding eighteen cases of false-positive results in tests involving truck drivers who had been taking large doses of White Cross pills to keep them awake on the road. Sold in pharmacies as a nonprescription nasal decongestant, the pills showed up as methamphetamine in the urine tests. Although improved technology has greatly reduced the risk of false-positives in recent years, the possibility of error remains.

The majority of large companies and all federal government agencies now perform confirmatory tests on initial positive results as well as a medical review of those that are confirmed. These secondary tests, which rely on more expensive, more precise technology, are specifically designed to verify the presence of drugs picked up in the preliminary screening. They achieve near-perfect accuracy. However, smaller companies are often reluctant to assume the expense of additional testing, which increases the risk that job applicants and employees may be falsely identified as illicit drug users. Although aggrieved workers have recourse to the courts, where earlier litigants have succeeded in obtaining job reinstatement and damages, lawsuits are often lengthy and costly, which may well discourage some individuals from seeking vindication. To reduce the possibility of error, increasing numbers of states now require all employers who conduct testing to provide confirmation of initial positive results.[7]

Two-thirds of the largest U.S. companies (those with 5,000 employees or more) conduct drug testing, compared to less than a third of all businesses nationwide. In the federal government, more than 2 million employees are subject to drug testing. In addition, the Department of Transportation requires testing of four million private transportation workers, including airline pilots, truck drivers, and railroad engineers, and the Department of Defense requires all defense contractors to establish comprehensive drug programs including testing.

Drug testing of job applicants is by far the most widespread type of screening. The U.S. military routinely tests new recruits, as do virtually all private companies that use any type of drug testing. IBM's Dr. Glen Houghie points out that "identifying drug users in the applicant pool saves a lot of expense and grief and more than pays for the costs of drug testing." The U.S. Postal Service estimates that screening out drug-using applicants from its 180,000-person workforce saves $105 million in turnover and absentee costs during their employment tenure.

Sometimes drug testing reveals unexpected—and unpleasant —truths about a company and its community. In 1988 Tropicana Orange Juice posted large signs outside the employment office at its Bradenton, Florida, headquarters, informing applicants that drug screening would be required starting that August. Walk-in applications plummeted 50 percent the first year. "We checked the doors of the employment office to make sure they weren't locked!" recalls Martin Gutfreund. "An outside video camera showed people would come up to the office, read the sign, and turn around and leave."

Among those who actually came in the door, about a quarter tested positive, primarily for marijuana and cocaine. "It was an incredible eye-opener for us," Gutfreund says. "We had to come to grips with the fact that our workforce is a real cross-section of society. But we also learned that the stereotype of drug abuse as being predominantly a minority problem is wrong. On the TV news, you only see blacks in big-city drug busts—you never see secretaries and salesmen. But we found that two-thirds of the people testing positive were white, even though our applicant pool has a higher percentage of minorities than the general population."

Most companies permit applicants who test positive to reapply for employment. IBM requires a six-month waiting period before reapplication, and a second positive test bars any future employment. Tropicana also allows reapplication after six months. Unlike many companies which do not inform applicants why they have been rejected, Tropicana tells them they have tested positive for drugs. "We look people right in the eye and ask them if they want to talk about their drug use," Gutfreund explains. "Our intention is to call this problem to their attention so that we don't pretend it's not there."

The percentage of applicants testing positive has declined substantially at all companies. Positive pre-employment drug tests at Southern California Edison dropped from 26.5 percent in 1985 to less than 1 percent in 1990. Drug positives among Johnson & Johnson applicants dropped from 5 percent in 1987 to about 1 percent three years later. During the same period, Capital Cities/ABC—the only television network to require pre-employment testing—reported declines from 11 percent to 5 percent. "The word is out that if you want to work here you're going to be tested," says Charles Keller, "so a certain percentage don't even bother to apply. At some of our newspapers with high-turnover jobs, people just walk out when they see the sign saying that drug testing is a precondition of employment."

Pre-employment testing has generally proved effective in screening out applicants who use drugs. Charles Neilson, vice president for human resources at Texas Instruments, thinks pre-employment testing is "a kind of IQ test: Since every applicant knows he's going to be tested, he can't be too bright if he fails." Dr. Louis Cardi, director of corporate health affairs at Johnson & Johnson, believes that job applicants who now test positive for cocaine are "probably hooked, since they know they have to pass a drug screen which shows whether they've taken cocaine in the past forty-eight hours. Otherwise they could plan ahead and stop using cocaine two days before the test."

As pre-employment testing becomes common practice, pressure builds on nontesting companies to protect themselves against applicants who are not willing or able to pass drug tests. Because of this, several major California banks were poised to begin pre-employment drug testing in late 1991. Then the California Court of Appeals ruled that psychological screening of job applicants violated their right to privacy, suggesting that drug testing may also be unconstitutional. In a 1994 decision, the California Supreme Court found that drug testing of intercollegiate athletes did not violate their privacy, opening the way for broader pre-employment testing. Nonetheless, the California banks have decided not to go ahead with their plan, in large part to limit expenses.

■

Drug tests of employees on the job are generally conducted "for cause" after accidents or if a supervisor notices erratic behavior, absenteeism, or other performance problems which might be linked to drug use. Most companies provide special training to help supervisors recognize symptoms of drug use. Even so, giving supervisors responsibility for deciding whom to test can lead to employee harassment. To reduce this possibility, some companies, like IBM, leave the ultimate decision up to the medical division, while others, like Tropicana, require three independent observations of employee behavior. Although initially challenged by labor unions as violating Fourth Amendment protections against unreasonable searches and seizures, for-cause testing was upheld by the U.S. Supreme Court in 1989.

Random testing, which tests employees without advance warning, is by far the most controversial use of drug testing.

The federal government requires random testing of workers whose jobs affect public health, safety, and national security— about 400,000 employees in 1991. Implementation of the testing program has been slowed by legal challenges, so that only a quarter of the total were tested in 1990. Random testing is very limited in the private sector, involving fewer than 10 percent of companies which conduct any kind of drug testing.

IBM, for example, uses random testing only to monitor employees who return to safety-sensitive jobs after being treated for drug and alcohol problems. Johnson & Johnson uses random testing more extensively, including all employees in jobs which affect the public safety, such as vehicle drivers, chemical manufacturers, and salespeople. Although the unions threatened to strike when Johnson & Johnson instituted random testing, they changed their position when management held firm. "When you talk to the rank and file, they're worried about their own safety. They knew who was going out to the bathroom to use drugs and they wanted it stopped," Dr. Cardi recalls. "The union leadership now reluctantly accepts this, particularly since we protect confidentiality and offer comprehensive treatment for those who test positive."

Concerns that random testing violates employees' rights to privacy have led to strict legal requirements in more than a dozen states. California, for example, allows employers to test only on the basis of "reasonable suspicion" of drug use based on measurable work impairment. In 1989 the U.S. Supreme Court upheld random testing of public employees in highly safety-sensitive positions, such as armed law enforcement officials and Customs officials involved in drug interdiction.

The discriminatory possibilities raised by random testing are largely eliminated in a new program developed by Texas Instruments. "Universal random testing" tests all employees "from the chairman of the board to the newest engineer," explains

Charles Neilson, who has himself been tested several times since the program began in late 1989. Although Texas Instruments has screened job applicants for drugs since 1985, the broader employee testing program was developed in response to Department of Defense regulations requiring contractors to adopt antidrug policies, including testing. "We realized it didn't make any sense just to test those employees working on government contracts, so we decided to include everyone. Our employees told us that they didn't mind being tested if their bosses were tested first," Neilson recalls.

Today less than 1 percent of Texas Instruments' employees test positive. "This is a very high-profile program which says very clearly that we don't accept drugs in our workplace," Neilsen explains. "Before we began, we always had two or three drug investigations going on in our plants, but now that has all stopped."

Employees who test positive are referred to treatment through the employee assistance program and are tested twice again in the eight months following treatment. A second positive test results in dismissal. Thus far, very few employees have been let go. A survey of the company's 50,000 employees in 1990 found that three-quarters think the program is fair, largely because it applies equally to everyone and does not depend on the discretion of managers.

Unlike many other large companies, Texas Instruments almost never conducts for-cause testing, which Neilson points out "sounds super, but in reality doesn't work very well. Either you get overzealous supervisors who grab everyone for testing, especially young people with a different life-style or minorities, or you get supervisors who are so afraid of making a mistake they don't recommend testing very often." When employees behave erratically, their supervisors refer them to the EAP rather than order drug testing.

Consistent with its policy of universal testing, Texas Instruments requires contract employees who work in company facilities to undergo testing, both as a means of maintaining a drug-free workplace and out of fairness to the regular employees. The company also provides technical assistance to other companies on setting up universal testing programs.

Motorola began universal random drug testing of its 60,000 employees in 1991, based on the Texas Instruments model. Although Motorola had been conducting pre-employment and for-cause testing since 1987, the company decided that universal testing would significantly reduce costs. "Motorola's culture demands excellence and a top-quality workforce," explains Donald Cramer, assistant corporate director for employee relations. "Several years ago when Roger Smith announced that drug use was costing General Motors $1 billion a year, we figured out that meant about $150 to $200 for each car they produced. These kinds of costs sure put a dent in your competitive edge." Cramer estimates that Motorola's universal testing program costs about $600,000 a year but believes that savings in medical expenses, productivity, and reduced absenteeism will more than pay for it.

The consequences of testing positive can be severe. Southern California Edison imposes a "two-strike" rule on nuclear power plant workers. The positive drug test leads to a fourteen-day suspension, mandatory rehabilitation, and subsequent drug testing. A second positive test results in dismissal. Johnson & Johnson also allows employees a second chance and dismisses those who test positive after returning from treatment. More than half of J & J's employees referred to treatment through the EAP since 1987 have stayed off drugs. The rest either have left the company or have switched into jobs in which testing is not required.

Tropicana Orange Juice takes a very tough approach involving widespread random, for-cause, and pre-promotion testing. Any employee who tests positive is fired automatically. "How can you have a war on drugs without a few casualties?" asks Martin Gutfreund. "Firing is an important deterrent, and some employees learn from the experience of others. We couldn't run this kind of program without the support of our workers and the local Teamsters, our largest union. They know that maintaining a drug-free workplace is key to their safety and the well-being of the business."

■

Drug testing is strongly supported by the public. A 1989 Gallup poll found that two-thirds of American workers favor it for themselves and over 90 percent support the testing of workers in safety-sensitive jobs.[8]

But drug testing has serious limitations. Even the most reliable tests are not foolproof, and individuals who falsely test positive face potentially disastrous consequences. Although an initial error may be corrected through secondary tests, the stigma of being identified as an illegal drug user may be hard to erase.

Even when tests are accurate, they show only that drugs were recently used. They do not reveal whether the person is an occasional user or a chronic abuser. For-cause tests, which are given after an accident or if an employee is behaving erratically, do not necessarily measure work impairment. Although urine tests can detect marijuana use up to two weeks earlier, they may not explain an employee's work performance on a particular day.

As might be expected, drug users have become sophisticated in beating the tests. A recent study of intercollegiate athletes subject to mandatory drug testing found that some successfully avoided detection by taking diuretics, drinking large amounts of water, and using certain foods and drinks to disguise drugs in the urine.[9]

But new technology may soon overtake drug testing's central role in detecting possible performance problems. Dr. Ensor Rodriguez, medical director of ARCO, predicts that within five years, three-minute computer games will be widely available which measure a worker's capacity to concentrate on the task at hand. "If we're looking for the common denominator of safety, drug and alcohol use are a drop in the bucket compared to stress, illness, and fatigue," Dr. Rodriguez explains. "These new computer tests will give us more bang for the buck because they screen out workers who could cause accidents as well as identify possible drug and alcohol problems which can then be confirmed in secondary testing."

Objective computer tests administered routinely to the entire workforce would greatly reduce the possibility of discrimination against certain workers. They would measure a much broader range of impairment than drug tests, and be far more effective in protecting the public safety, improving productivity, and reducing absenteeism. Employee problems with stress, illness, fatigue—and drugs and alcohol—would be addressed in the larger medical context, through EAPs or private physicians, removing much of the stigma now associated with positive drug-test results.

■

Drug-free workplace programs are still largely restricted to the nation's largest companies, but the vast majority of Americans work in businesses which employ fewer than fifty people. Only 10 percent of these smaller firms provide employee assistance programs and fewer than 3 percent require drug testing.[10] Small business owners often don't believe that drug use affects their bottom line, since they usually know their employees personally. Yet, as testing becomes widespread at larger companies, small businesses are increasingly the employer of last resort for substance abusers.

Initiatives to persuade small businesses to adopt antidrug programs have recently started in a number of communities. In Miami, Business Against Narcotics and Drugs (BAND) sent out volunteers to talk with employers about tailoring drug policies to suit their needs, providing a step-by-step guide on setting up workplace programs. "We couldn't recruit many small employers at first, but when we started asking if their insurance premiums were going up, we got their attention," recalls Sun Bank's Thomas Van Etten, one of BAND's organizers. "These guys are worried about meeting payrolls, so they need to see how drug programs will save them money."

BAND negotiated successfully with EAP providers and drug-testing labs to provide services to smaller businesses at the same rates paid by high-volume purchasers. At the same time, Tropicana Orange Juice donated $175,000 to the Florida State Chamber of Commerce to provide matching grants to fifteen local chambers to start BAND programs. Through this initiative, small businesses in Florida can now buy annual EAP coverage for $14 per employee and drugs tests for $20 each.

"Who can afford not to participate?" says Martin Gutfreund. "This is the greatest positive investment we've ever made at Tropicana. Avoiding the costs of one accident more than pays for drug testing and EAP coverage for the entire year. And now through the BAND program, small companies can have the same benefits we do."

Tropicana, the largest employer in Manatee County, has succeeded in recruiting 470 local businesses, about 40 percent of the county's total workforce, to join BAND. Tropicana employees are urged to shop at businesses which display the special BAND decal. Manatee County businesses now use BAND membership as a marketing tool. Local moving companies, for example, advertise that their employees are drug-free to convince customers that their possessions will be handled with care.

Tropicana also started a "preferred vendor" program to encourage their suppliers to adopt drug-free workplace programs. "We are using our economic leverage as creatively as possible to get drugs out of the workplace," Gutfreund explains. "When a company establishes strong antidrug policies, it communicates a set of values which affects everyone from management to line workers and shapes the larger culture of the community. If we're going to make America truly competitive, we don't think there is really any other choice."

Similarly, in Washington, D.C., the Corporation Against Drug Abuse (CADA) began a Small Business Project in 1991 to promote drug-free workplace policies and programs among the 97,000 metropolitan area businesses with fewer than one hundred employees. With support from the Robert Wood Johnson Foundation, CADA created a model small employer consortium which can be replicated in other cities.[11]

■

We have learned that the workplace, like the community, can organize effectively to drive out illegal drugs. Companies which have adopted strong antidrug programs point to reduced absenteeism, lower turnover, and substantial declines in positive drug tests as evidence of their success. While businesses have chosen different approaches tailored to fit their corporate cultures, certain themes are common to all. Effective workplace programs not only change the way people behave on the job but also shape their attitudes toward drugs. Providing immediate, confidential assistance for employees with drug problems speeds recovery as well as affirms the employer's commitment to taking action against drug abuse. Drug testing, as part of a comprehensive program which respects individual rights and applies equally to labor and management, can be a useful tool in encouraging drug abusers to seek treatment. When employees know that their jobs depend on kicking the habit—and are also able to find help through readily accessible treatment programs—they are much more likely to succeed in giving up drugs than those without these supports.

7.

Treating Addiction

Americans still tend to view addiction as a moral problem and treatment as a one-shot effort, where success depends largely on willpower.[1] A relapse is seen as a complete failure rather than a temporary setback. By contrast, the public understands that overcoming addiction to alcohol and tobacco usually requires repeated attempts. A former drinker who occasionally "falls off the wagon" or a smoker who tries several times to "kick the habit" receives far more support than a drug user experiencing the same difficulties.

Dr. Richard Rawson, a psychiatrist who has successfully treated hundreds of cocaine addicts at his Matrix program in Beverly Hills, believes that "treatment designed as a single episode doesn't reflect the reality of addiction as a chronic, relapsing condition. It's not like taking out an appendix; it's more like working with someone who has high blood pressure to bring it under control. Treatment is a continuing process which takes sustained effort over time."

Many Americans believe that most addicts wouldn't want treatment even if it were available. This belief persists despite overwhelming evidence that when treatment becomes accessible and affordable, drug abusers do seek help. Dr. Robert Millman, director of Drug and Alcohol Abuse Services at New York Hospital–Cornell Medical Center, points out that almost all addicts want to be free of their dependence on drugs. "The pleasure drugs provide wears out very quickly, as the euphoric high is replaced by painful withdrawal symptoms or insatiable craving," says Dr. Millman. "What often begins as a social activity turns into grim isolation as the addict loses self-respect, family, and friends in pursuit of his all-consuming drug habit."

Some people believe that drug addicts do not deserve treatment, especially if taxpayers' dollars must pay for it. Naya Arbiter, director of Amity, a therapeutic community program in Tucson, Arizona, thinks that most Americans view addicts as "throw-away people" who should be ignored or locked up. "So much of this war on drugs has been spent identifying and rejecting the enemy, deepening the division between 'us' and 'them,' " she observes. "Once we make drug addicts into the enemy, society has a tough time taking them back in. Why would the public want to pay for more treatment if they're dealing with the enemy? It's not surprising that Arizona is fourth in the country in per capita expenditures for prisons and last on drug treatment."

Treatment was a declining priority nationwide throughout the 1980s, as drug enforcement came to dominate state and federal spending. In 1993 treatment received 19 percent of the $12.2 billion federal drug budget compared to 25 percent twelve years earlier, well before the cocaine epidemic created millions of new addicts. The impact of this shift in priorities is painfully obvious in most cities, where addicts often face waits of three months or longer before they can get help.[2]

Judge Herbert Klein, who in 1989 helped create Miami's special court for drug offenders, maintains that what we need is a change in attitudes about treatment. "We can't just write off large segments of society," he says. "Drug addiction is a disease which people are powerless to fight unless they have the tools. We have an obligation to give them those tools, and we know now that a large majority can be helped."

Most Americans don't realize that treatment indeed works, although not always, and often not the first time. Success rates are higher for people with stable families, employment, and outside interests, and lower for those who suffer from serious depression and who do not have solid opportunities. But the single most important key to success is length of time in treatment.[3] National studies which have followed tens of thousands of addicts through different kinds of programs report that one-third of those who stay in treatment longer than three months are still off drugs a year later. The success rate jumps to two-thirds when treatment lasts a year or longer.

Initial dropout rates when addicts first enter treatment are high, which contributes to the public perception that treatment doesn't work. At Detroit's Hutzel House, for example, which provides day treatment and prenatal care for pregnant addicts, more than half the women quit within the first three weeks. Phoenix House, the nation's largest therapeutic community program, loses about a third of its clients within the first six weeks, but 80 percent of those who stay in treatment at least a year remain drug-free. The retention rate is often higher in methadone programs, where heroin addicts receive daily doses of oral methadone. At New York City's Beth Israel methadone maintenance treatment program, three-quarters of the 8,000 clients remain at least a year, and half stay for three years or longer.

Dr. Douglas Anglin, director of the Drug Abuse Research Center at the University of California at Los Angeles, believes that treatment success should be defined more broadly. "Many people assume that high dropout rates mean that treatment doesn't work, but research confirms that it does," Anglin explains. "Though some addicts may succeed in staying off drugs the first time they try, most will go in and out of treatment a number of times. Each time they do, their drug use goes down, along with their criminal activity. Even if they never achieve abstinence, they may be able to reduce the size of their habits, or shift to less harmful drugs. These are positive gains, both for the addict and society."

Nina Peyser, director of the Beth Israel program, points out that the public often uses a double standard to measure success, judging addicts who rely on public programs more harshly than those who can afford private treatment. "For professional people, the issue of repeated failure rarely comes up, " Peyser says. "But we expect impoverished drug addicts to pull themselves up by their bootstraps even though the reality of their lives is unemployment, lack of opportunity, and discrimination. Public programs don't have the funds or political support to address those needs. People often end up condemning treatment because it fails to bring addicts who have nothing to begin with into the middle class."

∎

The crack epidemic overwhelmed a public treatment system already seriously weakened by major federal funding cuts which began in 1981. Treatment programs were unprepared for the massive increase in the number of people needing help, particularly women and teenagers hooked on the most addictive drug in our history. Most treatment had been designed for adult male heroin addicts, usually in methadone maintenance programs or therapeutic communities requiring extended residential stays. Too few programs understood that the "new" cocaine addicts invariably abused a variety of drugs, including alcohol. And even fewer addressed the special needs of adolescents and women, particularly those with children. But in recent years, a number of new approaches have been developed which show good results.

One of the most effective nonresidential cocaine treatment programs is Matrix. Developed by Dr. Richard Rawson for wealthy cocaine abusers in Beverly Hills, Matrix is now being tested on thousands of poor and working-class crack addicts in Los Angeles. Early studies indicate that about 70 percent of the affluent Matrix group succeed in giving up drugs compared to 30 percent of poor, inner-city users.[4] Dr. Rawson points out that the rewards of abstinence are much greater for middle-class clients: "Once they're off cocaine, their personal and work lives improve dramatically and they have more money and leisure time to enjoy themselves. Most poor people do not have these reinforcers in the environment to sustain their behavior change, so relapse is more frequent." At the Watts Health Center, Matrix is working with community treatment organizations to develop supportive programs for recovering inner-city addicts. In New York City, the Matrix approach is being tried with pregnant crack addicts as well as methadone-maintained clients who continue to abuse cocaine.

What is distinctive about Matrix is its intense focus on helping the individual to understand the biological and psychological stages of cocaine recovery and to create a daily structure which will prevent relapse. During the first six months of treatment, clients attend more than half a dozen counseling sessions weekly and undergo regular urine tests. During the second six months, group meetings are held once a week with individual counseling and urine testing if needed.

Dr. Rawson believes that establishing new routines is critical in order to resist the many "cues" to return to cocaine that the recovering addict experiences in himself and his environment. "Keeping them coming in to treatment is the key to success. If I just wore a clown suit and roller skates and that worked, I'd do it," he explains. "Requiring our clients to attend more than one hundred sessions in six months teaches them they can have control over their lives. But we also work with them and their families to make sure there's a support system in place to channel the momentum they get from treatment into a workable, solid routine in their own lives."

At Matrix, the central goal is changing drug-using behavior, not finding the root causes of the addiction. "Treatment should be extremely supportive, so that the client looks forward to coming instead of dreading it," Dr. Rawson says. "Cocaine users feel completely out of control and don't understand their own behavior. They often don't come back if they think you're passing judgment on them, or don't know how to help them. Our therapists are trained to help the patient analyze his behavior regardless of what he reports. If he keeps using, we increase the intensity of treatment rather than throw him out of the program. We can try some of the experimental drugs, like desipramine and bromocriptine, to reduce cravings, or add Antabuse if drinking triggers a return to cocaine. And we can talk about residential treatment instead of outpatient care."

Since moving rapidly from addiction to abstinence may not be realistic for some people, Dr. Rawson believes that substantial improvements can be made short of full recovery. "It's a tough call when to say we can't help someone anymore. We have some very difficult patients who have tried many other kinds of treatment, like John R., a Hollywood agent, who has cut his cocaine use down from every day to twice a month since he's been at Matrix. I don't think we're 'enabling' his addiction; we're helping him get control over his life. Eventually, he may be able to give up cocaine completely, but kicking him out at this point won't teach him anything."

Another promising approach to cocaine treatment, the Manhattan Midtown Center for Treatment and Research, shares Matrix's relapse prevention techniques but makes greater use of intensive group therapy, peer interaction, and Alcoholics Anonymous–type meetings. Dr. Robert Millman, who developed the program in 1986, believes that many addicts have serious psychological problems—sometimes created by their drug use—which must be treated along with teaching them to modify their behavioral responses to the "cues" to return to drugs. Like Matrix, the program is most successful with employed clients who are strongly motivated to quit and least effective with those who have few external supports. But despite the positive results both Matrix and the Manhattan Center have with many cocaine and crack addicts, there are currently fewer than a dozen comprehensive nonresidential programs of this type in the country.

Acupuncture, one of the tools the Manhattan Center employs to help cocaine users overcome drug cravings, has gained widespread acceptance in treating addiction. Based on the ancient Chinese therapeutic practice of inserting very fine needles in key nerve centers, acupuncture treatment for heroin addicts was pioneered by Dr. Michael Smith at New York City's Lincoln Hospital in 1972. As crack addiction surged in the mid-1980s, a number of programs began experimenting with acupuncture. Although studies of its effectiveness are still limited, many drug users say they are helped by such sessions. The mechanisms of how acupuncture works are still not well understood, but it is widely believed that the needles stimulate the body to release chemicals which suppress the craving for drugs.

Miami's Model Cities Acupuncture Outpatient Clinic treats

more than two thousand drug offenders—virtually all of whom are crack addicts—referred by the city's Drug Court. During six months of intensive treatment, clients come to the clinic for daily acupuncture sessions, urine tests, and optional counseling. Two-thirds successfully complete this first phase and more than half continue through the second six months of treatment, which consists of acupuncture and urine tests twice a week. In the final phase of the program, clients attend educational and vocational courses at Miami-Dade Community College.

Raymond White, the clinic director, believes acupuncture changes the dynamics of treatment by offering addicts a concrete service. "All we had to give them in the past were words, and most of our clients are not verbal," he explains. "Acupuncture seems to alleviate cocaine withdrawal symptoms—hyperactivity, hostility, agitation, inability to sleep, loss of appetite. Our clients say they look forward to coming because they find the forty-five minutes of acupuncture so restful. I've never seen people go drug-free for such long stretches in an outpatient program."

The Hooper Detoxification Facility in Portland, Oregon, the first clinic in the country to use acupuncture as part of its residential program, also reports positive results. Before acupuncture was offered in 1987, 80 percent of the addicts dropped out before completing the weeklong detoxification program; now the dropout rate ranges from 10 to 20 percent. Hooper currently requires all incoming patients—alcoholics as well as cocaine and heroin addicts—to participate in daily acupuncture sessions. A comprehensive outpatient program at the Portland Addictions Acupuncture Center (PAAC), which treats over two hundred alcoholics and drug addicts daily, also offers acupuncture, along with group therapy, individual counseling, and AA and NA meetings.

David Eisen, a social worker and licensed acupuncturist who directs both Hooper's acupuncture clinic and PAAC, points out that acupuncture does not provide an instant cure but can be an immensely useful tool. "Acupuncture keeps people coming back," Eisen observes. "In our early morning clinic, you can see bankers in their three-piece suits sitting next to punk-rock teenagers and skid-row alcoholics. They all have needles in their ears and knees and contented smiles on their faces. Of course, that's only the first step. Many of them need jobs, housing, counseling, and the continuing support of AA and NA groups. But acupuncture helps us engage them in recovery."

Alcoholics Anonymous, Narcotics Anonymous, Cocaine Anonymous, and similar self-help groups provide continuing support for hundreds of thousands of recovering addicts and their families. Based on principles developed originally by Alcoholics Anonymous, these groups practice the "twelve steps" to recovery, which include admitting one's powerlessness over alcohol and drugs, surrendering to a higher power, admitting past harms to others, and attempting to make amends for them. The meetings, run by members of the fellowship who are also recovering, are open to anyone who wishes to participate and are held in churches, recreation centers, and hospitals all over the country. In New York City, for example, there are more than two thousand AA, CA, and NA meetings each week. While these programs are not useful for everyone, particularly those who resist the idea of surrendering to a higher power, they offer the support, inspiration, and structure many addicts desperately need as they rebuild lives free of drugs and alcohol.

At Detroit's Genesis I, a residential program for fifteen drug-addicted and homeless women and their children, participation in AA is the key to treatment and after-care. Kathy Addison, a Genesis counselor, explains that after completing the two-month program the women return to Detroit's inner city where they have very few supports: "Our women need AA meetings like an ill person needs medication. Back on the streets, they're surrounded by drugs and dealers. We take them food if they need it and help them however we can. But most of all they need to talk about what they are going through, get spiritual strength to hold on to their gains, and be with other people who are trying to develop a new life-style. Otherwise they weaken and relapse."

Recovering addicts with stronger economic supports than the women at Genesis I also find the fellowship of AA and similar "twelve-step" groups helpful. Some participants have already completed intensive outpatient programs like Matrix or have been treated by private doctors. Others spend a month or longer living at hospitals or clinics with specialized chemical-dependency programs staffed by recovering addicts and health care professionals.

These "rehabilitation programs" are informed by the view that addiction is a medical disease, not a moral weakness or psychiatric disorder. Patients participate in group and individual therapy, family sessions, and classes on the negative effects of drugs and alcohol and how to prevent relapse. AA meetings are central to the process. Recent studies report that those who complete one month of residential drug treatment and continue to attend AA-type meetings regularly are almost twice as likely to remain off drugs than those who do not attend the follow-up support sessions.[5]

■

David B., a physician and a recovering cocaine addict, attends AA meetings in Boston three times a week. A charming, articulate man in his late fifties, David was head of plastic surgery for twenty years at a large teaching hospital in New England. During his last six years as department chairman, he used cocaine daily.

"I realize now that the pattern of my life made me a dead duck for this disease," David recalls. "I worked all the time, always driving to success, but I was never really satisfied with what I had achieved. When my wife and I divorced ten years ago, I began to let go of some of the terrific control that had held the fabric of my life together. I started to socialize more. At one of the hospital parties, a friend offered me some cocaine. I loved it.

"Doctors have easy access to drugs, and a substantial number get in trouble, but they can often hide it pretty well. I used cocaine almost every night for six years—I had my own supplies at the hospital—and it kept me going without sleep. To help me come down, I started drinking vodka, several water glasses at a time. I continued to practice—and do complicated operations—but I was really coming apart."

Three years ago, David's children persuaded him to go to Minnesota for residential treatment at Hazleden, which has become a model for many rehabilitation programs. After a month at Hazleden, he returned home, and although he didn't lose his medical license, he was put on probation and monitored with regular urine tests. He had weekly therapy sessions with a psychiatrist and attended AA meetings every day.

"The AA meetings have opened up parts of me I never knew existed," David explains. "Whatever their background, whatever they've done, people can talk honestly about what's on their mind. No matter how much you achieve, you're really not much different from the next person. But it took me a long time and a lot of pain to learn that."

A year after David began attending AA, he met Karen J., who had been addicted to Valium and alcohol for ten years. "Karen managed to raise two kids after her husband left and put herself through business school," David says, "but one day she woke up in the emergency room after overdosing on Valium. She went into a residential program, and then came to AA. A group of us started going out for coffee after meetings. Karen and I got married last year. It's a whole new life for both of us. She's back at work and doing very well. My probation is up next month. Every day we're grateful we've found a second chance."

■

Some addicts find their second chance in therapeutic communities—highly structured, residential programs that last a year or longer.[6] Shaped by the view that substance abuse is caused by personality problems and inadequate social and educational skills, therapeutic communities work on changing the addict's vision of himself and the world through peer pressure, counseling, and group therapy.

Dr. Mitchell Rosenthal, president of Phoenix House, points out that most therapeutic community clients have long histories of disturbed behavior and drug abuse, yet many transform their lives in a relatively short time. "Through the power of the group—which becomes a replacement family—they learn the language of their inner lives, just as children do from their parents, sisters, and brothers," he explains. "They are able to connect their feelings with their actions, often for the first time, and see that they can change their lives."

Eric F., a resident of Phoenix House in Long Island City, New York, is a thirty-three-year-old recovering crack addict. He describes the journey that many others have taken: "After two years smoking crack, I lost everything—my wife, my three kids, my job. I went to prison for robbery. When I got out, I went right back to drugs. I was always alone. I never had a social network. One day it hit me, I'm dead already and I never had a life. I didn't know how to be a father, a husband, a man. I went through several detoxes before I decided to get my life together. I've been at Phoenix House for nine months, and I'm learning how to accept responsibility and rejection. I don't make excuses anymore. That life out there isn't going to change, but I see now that I can change."

Because therapeutic community programs are physically and psychologically rigorous, the dropout rate is very high. Only one in four clients remain longer than three months, while fewer than one in six complete the one- to two-year course of treatment. But among those who do stick it out, the success rate is high. A nationwide study in 1985 found that three-quarters of therapeutic community graduates were still drug-free seven years later. For those who drop out before completion, the overall success rate is lower, about one in three.[7]

To keep people in treatment, the Amity program in Tucson takes a less confrontational approach than some other therapeutic communities. Naya Arbiter, Amity's director, believes that "you can't terrify people into change. Addicts already think the worst about themselves, so putting dunce hats on them and making them do ridiculous, repetitive chores just reinforces their low self-image. Instead we try to pour love and respect into each other and keep creating community in larger and larger circles. Amity is really a place of the spirit, not of schedules."

Retention rates have tripled since 1980, and about 40 percent remain at Amity for at least a year. Although Amity (like most treatment programs) does not have funds to conduct formal follow-up studies, Arbiter estimates that more than three-quarters of Amity's graduates remain drug-free.

Amity emphasizes the importance of work—everyone has assigned daily responsibilities—and learning, with frequent group meetings to discuss philosophy, religion, literature, or other subjects. Special weeklong "retreats" for all residents are held five times a year to explore issues like racism, feminism, and criminal justice in America.

Robin McGrath, an Amity graduate who has been drug-free for nine years, recalls, "I woke up to life at Amity. They don't just go to group and talk about drug abuse. New materials are always being taught which help you understand who you are and what shapes you. I remember one retreat where we looked at Joseph Campbell's theories on the power of myth; suddenly I saw myself as part of a much bigger universe where there are so many things more interesting than drugs. Drug addicts usually don't have any interests that hook them to life, and drugs become a substitute for living."

Amity is one of the few residential programs where women's concerns play a key role. "Women make community happen by connecting people to each other," Arbiter says. "When you focus on women, as we do at Amity, it builds community for everyone and changes men's conception of themselves and their lives." Across the road from Amity's main buildings is an abandoned guest ranch, meticulously renovated by the residents, where a new program allows twenty women to live with their children while they are in treatment.

Amity brings together people from very different economic, social, and ethnic backgrounds, helping overcome the isolation of class and race. Half of Amity's residents are criminal offenders, referred by Arizona courts; about one-third are black, Hispanic, or Native American; and almost half are women. Some residents, like Carl R., the son of wealthy art dealers in New York City, pay $36,000 a year for treatment, while others who are unable to pay are taken free. Residents generally stay between one and two years. After they leave, they are encouraged to live together in Tucson for six months and stay involved in Amity, as well as participate in AA or NA meetings and do at least one month of volunteer community service. About half the staff are themselves Amity graduates.

At the heart of the recovery process at Amity and other therapeutic communities are frequent encounter groups where residents talk openly about their deepest feelings. Guided by an Amity counselor, these groups explore painful, explosive issues which many residents have previously avoided, often by taking drugs. The turning point comes when residents understand that their experiences have been shared by others. "Once they are able to talk about the things that are most difficult, they can face their own anger and shame," Arbiter explains. "Supported by the group, they then start to develop more positive relations with themselves and others. This process of breaking down years of denial and blame eventually leads to a new vision of life in which community and friendship overcome isolation, and the individual believes in the power to change."

■

In the "Power Room"—so named because of the powerful emotions that are released when Amity residents meet there—five women pull their chairs into a circle around a large wooden table made from a wagon wheel. In front of the stone fireplace are several brightly colored Indian rugs; the far wall is lined with books. Maryellen Heard, the group leader, is a small, energetic blonde from Houston, who began using heroin twenty years ago, when she was eighteen. "I grew up in a wealthy, socially prominent family who never seemed to have time for me. My feelings weren't important to them; I always felt shoved in a corner," she recalls. "I discovered heroin at the University of Texas, and for escape it was even better than drinking, which everybody did. Of course, my family was horrified—such a scandal! They could deal with a drunk, but not a junkie." Heard laughs at the memory. "Amity is a very special place where people genuinely care about each other. The 'process' we work on together illuminates our connectedness. By building bridges to each other we begin to heal the wounds we have carried since childhood. And we are all wounded, whether we're white or black, rich or poor."

She greets the other women with open affection, jumping up to hug Amy N., who has just returned from several days at the local hospital for treatment of a lung infection. "I'm so glad to be back," Amy exclaims. "Being in the hospital reminded me of the twenty-eight-day drug rehabs where you sit and wait for the doctors to cure you. I used to feel so lonely in those places; my parents never came to visit. My dad is a pillar of the community back in Greenwich, but he's a closet drinker and just doesn't want to recognize what's going on with his kids."

Maria H., a tall Hispanic woman in her late twenties, interjects, "That sounds like my family, except for the pillar-of-the-community part. My dad was never around, but when he was, it was real bad. When he and his brothers started drinking they got nasty—when I was thirteen, two of my uncles raped me, and no one did anything about it. They all pretended nothing had happened. I started using heroin after that; I just wanted to escape."

The other women nod sympathetically. Heard reminds them that most women who become drug addicts have a history of being sexually abused and molested, but the memories are so painful they often block them out. "But that which hurts you the most can also heal you," she says. "Once we are able to talk about these experiences, we can help begin to help each other deal with them."

Trudy C., a black woman hunched inside a leather jacket, shouts angrily, "I'm so sick of hearing about healing. You can't heal some things, you just have to put them aside. I've been raped, too, once in prison by a guard, and five times by my mother's different boyfriends. That was before I moved out on my own."

Heard asks, "What did you want your mother to do? Not let bad things happen? Protect you?" Trudy begins to cry, wiping her eyes with a crumpled handkerchief which Maria has handed her. "Where was she when I needed her? Out drinking and carrying on. I might as well not have existed as far as she was concerned. I know I'll be wasting my time to go back and look at all that with my mother. She's not going to change," Trudy says.

Paula S., whose blue eyes have filled with tears, whispers, "I still feel like a bad little girl, like I'm being punished, whenever I think about my dad fooling around with me. But I'm a thirty-two-year-old woman," she says defiantly. "When my baby was stillborn last year I went back to heroin, I just couldn't stand the sadness. Do you ever get past being the little kid who is always getting hurt?"

"After a while you handle it differently, but it still comes up," Heard answers. "You've been here, off drugs, for eight months, and you know that you have to get out of the victim role. The only way to do that is to shine light on your pain and stop running from it, which means forgiving and healing."

Trudy says quietly, "My mom's life wasn't great either. Her mom used to wear switchblades in her hair and hang out in bars. She was raped, too, and gave the baby up for adoption. Then she got pregnant with my mom but the guy used to beat her up so bad she'd go to the hospital for stitches. So maybe my mom didn't know how to do better with me."

Maria asks her, "Aren't your two kids coming to live with you here next month?"

Trudy nods, "Yeah, I've been working hard fixing up our room, but I'm really scared. I don't want to be like my mom was with me. I want to find a job to take care of them, and make a nice home for us. But maybe I won't know how."

"You don't have to have all the answers," Amy says. "It's OK to look back and see who's hurt us and who we've hurt —we're really safe here."

"Besides, you've got us," Maria adds. "I'm counting on coming over and baby-sitting some evenings while you go to class. My own kids were put up for adoption five years ago when I was smoking so much crack, and I don't know where they are now. I've got a lot of love to give."

Trudy smiles and says to Maria, "I'm beginning to believe there may be a new day. Now, how's that coming from one crazy, angry black woman?"

The bell outside the dining hall rings and the women get up to go to lunch. As they walk out, talking quietly with each other, Heard adds, "The friends we make here really are our higher power; through them we can go back and learn how to trust and help others. It's those bonds which give us the hope and energy to begin again and live without drugs."

■

When other kinds of treatment have not worked for heroin addicts, methadone maintenance provides an effective alternative. Developed during World War II as a synthetic substitute for morphine, methadone was first used to maintain heroin addicts in 1964 by Drs. Vincent Dole and Marie Nyswander at New York City's Rockefeller University. It is now the most commonly used treatment for heroin addiction in the United States; only one-fifth of the nation's estimated 500,000 to 700,000 heroin addicts are currently in methadone programs.[8]

Programs vary considerably, depending on funding. Some are able to offer extensive counseling and health care in addition to methadone, but severe budget cutbacks have forced many other programs to reduce services. As a result, the quality of treatment and supervision has suffered in some places. Reports of occasional methadone diversion have reignited public concerns about methadone treatment. However, unlike heroin, methadone has limited value on the black market, appealing to heroin addicts who want to reduce their dependence on heroin but who are unable or unwilling to get treatment. In recent years, black-market demand for methadone has risen because of federal regulations mandating limits on methadone dosage and duration of treatment, causing some addicts in methadone programs to supplement their dosage with illegal purchases. But limiting the availability of methadone is self-defeating, since it makes methadone treatment more difficult for addicts without offering them adequate drug-free treatment alternatives. If methadone were freely available to heroin addicts, its black-market value would drop sharply.

Methadone has been evaluated more extensively than any other type of drug treatment and has demonstrated its effectiveness in reducing heroin use and criminal activity. Nationwide, more than two-thirds of methadone patients remain in treatment for at least two years and over 85 percent of those who remain on methadone stay off heroin for good. They also reduce their cocaine and alcohol use by 30 to 40 percent.

Studies of six methadone programs in Baltimore, New York, and Philadelphia in 1986 found that addicts in treatment longer than six months reported committing crimes an average of 24 days a year, compared to 307 days a year when addicted to heroin. In addition, methadone patients are more frequently employed and pursuing education than are heroin addicts.[9]

For many heroin addicts who are unable to kick the habit, methadone can be a lifelong treatment. Beth Israel's Nina Peyser, who has worked with methadone patients since 1975, points out that "many heroin addicts really have no choice physiologically. We don't yet understand the brain chemistry, but extensive research already indicates that there is some kind of metabolic disorder here. Almost all our patients have tried other kinds of treatment, but nothing worked. Talking therapy just doesn't help them. Methadone does."

For Margaret C., a thirty-seven-year-old housewife in Brooklyn, methadone has made the difference between life and death. "I began using drugs when I was twelve. By the time I was sixteen I was shooting heroin, living in the streets, really down and out. I've been on methadone since I was twenty, and it's kept me on the road. If it hadn't been for the program I'd be dead," she explains. "Now I'm on the board of the PTA at my daughter's elementary school. I go shopping, take care of the house, love my family—my life looks as normal as anyone else's. No one knows I'm on methadone, not even my daughter."

Margaret's husband has been on methadone for twelve years and has worked for the Transit Authority as a repairman for the past eleven years. They talk about getting off methadone, but Margaret is frightened she will go back to heroin. "I've detoxed from methadone three times in the past eighteen years. Once I stayed clean for six months, but I always ended up back on drugs. I've tried Phoenix House and two other therapeutic communities, but I don't like talking in groups. My counselors at the methadone program are wonderful; I know they would do anything to help me. But it's still a fight not to buy drugs. Each day I thank God for getting through it."

■

Although there is no single answer for curing drug abuse, we have learned a great deal about what works in treating heroin and cocaine addiction. We know that treatment must be lengthy—at least three months and preferably a year or more. We know intensive, highly structured treatment helps recovering addicts build new patterns of living without drugs. Holding onto these gains after leaving treatment often requires continuing participation in AA or other support groups that provide sustaining friendships with other recovering addicts. Educational, vocational, and employment opportunities also speed recovery, as we have learned from the substantially higher success rates among educated, affluent addicts. Waking up to life—as Robin McGrath did at Amity—is at the heart of the transformation that many recovering addicts experience. Discovering that there are avenues open to them that are more rewarding and less destructive than drugs is a powerful motive for change.

Since we do not yet understand the causes of addiction—whether biochemical deficiencies, psychological disorders, behavioral problems, or some combination are responsible—exploring many different approaches to treatment makes sense. Experimental drugs may hold promise for reducing the craving for cocaine or blocking its effects, as methadone does for heroin. Acupuncture eases drug withdrawal and clearly helps retain addicts in treatment. Therapeutic communities with their strong emphasis on encounter groups are effective for some, while others do better in outpatient programs which provide counseling, regular urine testing, and a variety of services. Matching the person to the right kind of program can greatly improve treatment effectiveness.[10]

Treatment programs should be "user friendly," designed to attract and retain addicts. Programs which allow women to live with their children, as they do at Amity, not only treat the mothers' drug problems but also teach them parenting skills which can break the cycle of addiction, abuse, and neglect passed from one generation to the next. Treatment and prevention converge when the children of drug abusers are able to grow up in a safe and caring community.

Thinking about treatment more comprehensively requires that we be more realistic about the criteria for success. Reducing the harmful consequences of addiction should be considered a positive gain even if complete abstinence is not achieved. By this measure, methadone maintenance is immensely successful, even though it substitutes one addiction for another. After they are stabilized on methadone, addicts are much less likely to commit crimes and are more able to hold down jobs and attend school. In the same way, bringing a cocaine addict's life under better control by reducing the size of his habit should not be viewed as failure but as progress on the road to recovery. The benefits to the country of expanded treatment are substantial. A 1990 study by the National Academy of Science's Institute of Medicine found that even the most expensive programs more than pay for themselves in reducing the costs of lost productivity, crime, and health care.[11]

Although we know now that treatment, like prevention, can work, we have not made it a top priority in the war on drugs. America still believes that law enforcement is a more effective weapon. In the criminal justice system, which currently has authority over 4.6 million offenders, the concentration of drug addicts is the greatest. Yet treatment is particularly scarce, reaching fewer than 15 percent of the estimated 1.38 million criminal offenders with serious drug problems.[12] Without treatment, these addicts continue to commit crimes to support their habits, returning again and again to fill the nation's courts and prisons.

8

■

Treating Criminal Offenders

Since our primary strategy in dealing with drug abuse is law enforcement, it is not surprising that the criminal justice system has been deluged with drug offenders. In the past decade, arrests for drug crimes more than doubled. At the same time, public frustration with escalating drug crime led to tougher laws, longer sentences, and the death penalty for major traffickers.[1] The most extreme example of this trend occurred in 1986, when a Detroit judge sentenced a forty-year-old man to life imprisonment without parole for possession of slightly more than one pound of cocaine. The offender had no previous criminal record, but the Michigan law gave the judge no discretion to take individual circumstances into account. The U.S. Supreme Court upheld the sentence in 1991, declaring that the Michigan law was not "cruel and unusual."[2]

The number of drug offenders currently serving prison sentences has doubled since 1985.[3] As a result, the nation's prisons are stretched far beyond capacity. In 1994 forty states and the District of Columbia were under court orders to relieve overcrowding. Some violent prisoners are released early in order to accommodate drug offenders who cannot be paroled.[4] Judge Stanley Goldstein, who presides over the Miami Drug Court, believes that "throwing away the key on small-time drug dealers is not the way to protect the public. It's very expensive to keep these guys locked up the rest of their lives. Our prisons are so overcrowded, we end up releasing really violent guys doing time for robbery or assault to make room for the others." As a result, Florida has the highest rate of prison admissions in the country but the shortest length of stay, which in 1989 averaged less than one year.

Additional pressure for prison space comes from parole violators.[5] Drug abuse is a major factor. When parolees test positive for drugs or miss appointments with their parole officers (often because they are on drug binges), they are arrested for violating the conditions of parole and sent back to prison.

Our reliance on law enforcement to curtail drug abuse is costly. New York State, for example, spent $2.1 billion for new prisons from 1983 to 1992, while the prison population doubled. Almost half of all current inmates have been convicted of drug felonies, compared to only 11 percent in 1982. But despite the substantial expansion in prison capacity, corrections officials project that by 1995, New York's prisons will again be severely overcrowded.[6]

California's prison population quadrupled during the 1980s to more than 120,000. As a result of a recent $3.2 billion prison construction program, California will be able to house 37,000 additional prisoners. But by the end of 1994 prisons will be operating at 150 percent of capacity, according to recent estimates by the California Commission on Inmate Population

Management. Although the state's prison expenditures have increased 200 percent since 1984, violent crime continues to climb.[7]

■

In the past decade, American taxpayers have voted billions of dollars to build more prisons without asking whether what happens inside the prison walls justifies their investment. While locking up drug offenders keeps them off the streets, it does not keep them off drugs. Drug use is widespread in many prisons, often with the tacit knowledge of prison authorities. Drugs are smuggled in by visiting relatives as well as by guards who sell directly or take a percentage of the inmate dealers' profits.

Nor does the threat of rearrest deter addicts from using drugs or committing crimes after they are released from prison. Offenders with the most serious drug problems report committing hundreds of crimes each year, including robbery, burglary, and drug dealing. Without treatment, the majority return to crime and drugs after prison and are rearrested within three years.[8]

Yet treatment is still scarce in the criminal justice system. The General Accounting Office (GAO) reported in 1991 that only 364 of the 41,000 federal prison inmates who have substance abuse problems are participating in intensive treatment. More than three-quarters of all state prison inmates are substance abusers—at least 500,000 offenders—but only 10 to 20 percent receive any help. The GAO concluded that most prison treatment, which usually consists of occasional drug education and counseling, is ineffective.[9]

The lack of treatment comes in part from America's ambivalence toward "treating" criminals even when their crimes are directly related to addiction, and Americans are reluctant to approve any additional spending for the already costly criminal justice system. But Americans are also pessimistic that nothing works. In recent years, however, a number of programs have quietly shown good results. Within prisons, intensive drug treatment for inmates the year prior to release can reduce subsequent rearrest rates by one-third to one-half.

■

The model for effective prison programs is Stay'n Out, a therapeutic community which since 1977 has treated over 1,500 inmates in two New York State prisons, the Arthur Kill Correctional Facility for male offenders on Staten Island and the Bayview Correctional Facility for female offenders in Manhattan. Housed separately from the rest of the prison population, participants are supervised not by corrections officers but by program staff who are themselves recovered addicts and former offenders. Through intensive counseling, encounter sessions, and group seminars, the yearlong program encourages greater self-awareness, confidence, discipline, and respect for authority. Participants are initially assigned low-level jobs, like janitorial and dishwashing duties, and earn increased responsibility through hard work and involvement in the program. After release, as many as half the group continues treatment in residential programs in the community. Controlled evaluations of Stay'n Out have found that rearrest rates for program graduates three years after their release are one-third lower than for inmates who did not participate in the program.[10]

The Cornerstone program, located on the grounds of the Oregon State Hospital in Salem, is a therapeutic community for thirty-two prison inmates modeled on Stay'n Out. Participants have long histories of drug abuse; most have served over seven years in prison, with an average of seven felony convictions apiece. Gary Field, who has directed the program since 1982, estimates that 80 percent of the state's 6,000 prison inmates have serious substance abuse problems and that at least half would participate if treatment were available. But Oregon provides only 183 residential drug and alcohol treatment slots for prisoners.

Cornerstone also has a six-month after-care program. Graduates live in a halfway house and are assisted in finding housing, employment, education, and continuing treatment. "A good residential program can be no better than the after-care that follows," Field says. "Unless we help retrain our clients to live successfully in the community, whatever gains we make in here are quickly lost outside."

Two major evaluations of Cornerstone found much lower arrest, conviction, and incarceration rates among program graduates three years after release than among untreated inmates. During that period, almost half the Cornerstone group had not been convicted of any crime, compared to one-quarter of the untreated group. Length of time in treatment was strongly related to declines in recidivism.

Successful prison programs share certain common features. They have a separate living area for inmates participating in treatment, apart from the main prison population, as well as enthusiastic, well-trained staff who serve as role models. Treatment lasts at least six months to a year, usually immediately prior to release. Prerelease planning and after-care once the inmate returns to the community are also essential. Although good programs use a combination of group therapy, individual counseling, and skills training, they all communicate a deep sense of faith that recovery is possible.

■

Thirty men live in a separate wing of the new Pima County Jail in Tucson, Arizona, where they participate full-time in the Amity program. Every day, women inmates come from another wing to join the activities. They work on art projects; they learn history, music, reading, and writing skills; and they attend frequent group sessions, supervised by staff members who are Amity graduates.

The jail program operates on the same principles that guide Amity's therapeutic community—that addicts must learn to build community, close friendships, and meaningful interests which will sustain them in a life without drugs. Most of them will live at Amity after they leave jail.

Bill G., a slender, soft-spoken man in his late twenties, served five years in the state prison for robbery before being released to a community supervision program. At one of his parole appointments a few months later, he tested positive for cocaine and then ran away. Picked up for violating parole, Bill is facing fifteen years in prison, which the judge suspended in order to send him to Amity.

"I began shooting heroin when I was twelve, and I've been doing drugs ever since. But until now, no one recognized my drug problem," Bill explains. "I've walked on a razor's edge all my life, but I've never gotten help. I've got a wife and four kids—a new baby girl born last week—and I want to turn my life around. I need to quit being so angry and learn how to deal with it instead of shooting drugs."

Christina F., a young woman with curly blond hair and tattoos on her arms, has been in jail for eight months, the last month as part of the Amity program. She, too, has a long history of drug addiction. After being paroled from prison where she did time for burglary, she went on a drug binge and failed to report to her parole officer. Picked up at her home address on a warrant, she is now facing another prison term for violating her parole.

"I've done eight years of hard time for four different felonies. I'm thirty-one years old; I know this is the last chance for me. I want to be able to raise my little boy and have a regular home," she says. "After I got through high school, I worked for Hughes Aircraft as a secretary, but that seems so long ago. Amity is the first time I've really tried to clean up. But I still don't trust myself. I'm just taking it day by day."

Christina hopes to move into Amity's mothers and children program when space opens up. She will still be under court supervision, but she will be able to continue treatment and live with her seven-year-old son for the first time since he was a baby.

■

Naya Arbiter, Amity's director, points out that all the participants in the jail program have prior convictions, and many have been incarcerated two or three times. Some have been convicted for drug offenses, but many, like Bill and Christina, have committed other crimes. "Whatever they're in for is almost irrelevant, since it's their drug addiction that runs their lives," Arbiter explains. "But the correctional system rarely addresses the problem. They may violate them from parole for showing up with a dirty urine, but they don't provide the kind of intensive treatment necessary to help them restructure their lives."

In 1991 Amity was asked by the California Department of Corrections to establish a treatment program for 200 men inside the medium security R. J. Donovan correctional facility in San Diego. Most of California's 120,000 prison inmates have serious drug problems, but Amity's program at the Donovan facility is the only therapeutic community in the entire prison system.[11] Arbiter reports that "more than 1,500 men have already asked to participate in our program. When I walk through the cellblocks of the main prison and see all the inmates who need help, I feel as though I'm rowing a very small lifeboat. We can take so few and so many will be lost."

Therapeutic community programs in prison offer the greatest hope for drug offenders. In 1991 the National Task Force on Correctional Substance Abuse Strategies recommended establishing more residential treatment programs, noting that "the more firmly entrenched an offender is in terms of addiction and criminal life-style, the greater the intensity of services and supervision needed to begin the process of rehabilitation."[12] Stay'n Out costs about $4,000 a year above the $35,000 New York State pays to imprison one offender. Measured by the savings produced in reduced crime, these programs are clearly cost-effective. Yet despite their effectiveness, intensive residential programs are currently available for fewer than 6,000 prison inmates a year.

■

Faced with rising caseloads and overcrowded prisons, some criminal courts are finding new ways to keep drug offenders out of jail and in treatment. So far, these programs have succeeded in substantially reducing rearrest rates at a fraction of the cost of incarceration.

In California and Florida, special drug courts dispense a very personalized form of justice, using the threat of jail to prod offenders to enter treatment. Associate Chief Judge Herbert Klein of Florida's Eleventh Circuit Court, who helped create the Miami Drug Court in 1989, explains the rationale behind this judicial experiment: "We could get the numbers down by putting more and more offenders on probation, but that just perpetuates the problem. The same people are picked up again and again until they end up in the state penitentiary and take up space that should be used for violent offenders. The Drug Court tackles the problem head-on. We offer meaningful diversion where addicts can get treatment as well as social, educational, and vocational skills so they can find jobs."

The Drug Court handles all first-time felony drug possession cases in Miami, which exceed two thousand a year. At the time of arrest, defendants are given a choice between criminal prosecution with the possibility of going to jail or participating in the one-year treatment program. Judge Stanley Goldstein, who presides over the Drug Court, believes that making treatment immediately available is critically important. "In Miami, you really have to be tenacious to get into treatment," he observes. "Our programs have a six-month waiting list, and you have to telephone in every day or they take your name off the list. We knew we had to create our own treatment program or we'd lose those guys just at the moment when they're most likely to change." The program continues to work with those who relapse, but those who drop out of treatment are returned to the regular criminal court.

What makes the Drug Court extraordinary is Judge Goldstein's relationship with the defendants who come before him. A tough-talking former street cop and lawyer, Goldstein hands out praise, criticism, advice, and humor from the bench. To one young man who is completing his six-month treatment period, Goldstein says, "You're doing super. Look at you in that fine blue jacket and no drugs in your body. Come back in thirty days and let me know what your plans are."

To another, an eighteen-year-old cocaine addict who has violated probation on an earlier offense, Goldstein explains that he's going to keep him in the medical unit of the jail until space becomes available in a residential drug treatment program. "I know you don't want to be locked up, but if you fail now, you're facing three years in the state pen. I don't think you can handle going to a day treatment program, and I'm not going to let you screw up your whole life."

Goldstein says to the defendants still waiting their turn, "Listen to me, you all. You see some doing good and some doing lousy. They're no different from you. Just get out there and do it. Don't give me no jazz; I don't give up so easily, and if you fail, you're going right back to my hotel [the city jail]. It has a great view of downtown Miami, but no one wants to stay there even though it costs more than the Fontainebleu."

Goldstein believes that staying out of jail is a great motivator for getting treatment, but that close supervision is necessary. "In a sense, I'm their probation officer, but I'm not tied down by bureaucratic rules," he explains. "I operate on instinct and experience—and years and years out on the streets hearing every story in the book. Most judges only talk to lawyers, the prosecutor and the defense, but never get involved with the offenders themselves. It's not demeaning; it's the only way you get them to understand they can make real choices about their lives."

Two-thirds of the 4,500 defendants processed through Drug Court from June 1989 to April 1993 have successfully participated in treatment. (One-third drop out, disappear, or are re-arrested.) Among the 1,700 who have graduated from the program after a full year or longer, the rearrest rate is less than 3 percent. For those who have participated in treatment for shorter periods, the rearrest rate is 7 percent. This compares to rearrest rates of 30 percent for similar drug offenders who have not been through Drug Court.[13]

Drug Court also results in considerable savings. Keeping one offender in the Dade County jail for a year costs about $30,000, compared to $700 for each participant in the Drug Court treatment program. Judge Goldstein forcefully argues the case for the Drug Court's value: "Let me ask you a simple question.

Ten thousand people in Dade County have just lit up a rock. Are you going to put them all away? You can't hire that many cops, build that many prisons, and when you release them they go right back to what they were doing before. It's taking the taxpayers' money and flushing it down the toilet. Give me less money and I'll make it work better."

■

In Oakland, California, a similar approach has cut new arrests of drug offenders by half. Judge Jeffrey Tauber of Oakland Municipal Court, who began the diversion program in January 1991, maintains personal contact with first-time offenders, whom he requires to sign treatment contracts. Participants earn points for completing each stage of treatment, which can be used to reduce the two-year supervision period and fine. Unlike Miami, Oakland does not have a special treatment program for its drug court, but defendants must participate in AA and NA meetings, community counseling programs, intensive drug education classes, and frequent meetings with probation officers. Defendants are given random urine tests but those who relapse get a second chance. Because of reduced incarceration costs, Alameda County has saved over $2 million, and now rents empty jail cells to neighboring counties.[14]

"What we're doing is applying basic concepts of human behavior," Tauber explains. "We get people while they're in crisis and move very quickly to connect them to services and treatment. We let defendants know exactly what they have to do and what the rewards are for doing well. They also see the consequences of doing badly, when warrants are issued to pick up those who drop out and others are sent back to jail. I like to say to them that they are in control of their court case just like they're in control of their own lives."

The Miami and Oakland drug courts share common elements which contribute to their success. They process cases very quickly, seizing the moment after arrest to offer defendants real alternatives. They provide clear rewards and punishments as well as intensive treatment and supervision. They require frequent contact with authority in a very personal form—the tough but attentive judges who follow the participant's progress.

Drug experts believe that personalizing the judicial system makes a critical difference in changing offenders' behavior. Douglas Anglin, director of the Drug Abuse Research Center at the University of California at Los Angeles, points out that "it is very unusual for the criminal justice system to respond in a psychologically sound way. In addition to the serious consequences which the judge can impose for the offense, he also makes the whole process human. In these new drug courts, defendants can't just be passive recipients of punishment; they are propelled into becoming active participants in their own rehabilitation. They have to respond; they have to make choices. And because the judge is personally involved, a fair number of them end up wanting to earn his approval."

■

A new program begun in 1990 by the district attorney's office in Brooklyn, New York, combines residential treatment with tough enforcement for second-time felony offenders facing prison terms up to three years. Drug Treatment Alternative to Prison (DTAP) participants have all been arrested for selling drugs; more than 80 percent are addicted to heroin or cocaine. DTAP offers them the chance to live in therapeutic community programs run by Daytop Village, Samaritan Village, and Veritas in upstate New York. Those who complete treatment, which usually requires fifteen months to two years, will have the charges against them dismissed. Dropouts are picked up by a special enforcement team and returned to court for prosecution. The role of this enforcement team is explained before defendants decide to participate in the program. Whenever a dropout is returned to court, the other participants are told.

The retention rate after the program's first year is over 60 percent. Ninety-five percent of those who ran away or were expelled from the program have been returned to court for prosecution. The recidivism rate for program graduates is 8 percent, compared to 40 percent for offenders who serve prison sentences.[15] Susan Powers, the deputy district attorney who directs the program, believes that the high retention rate reflects the power of legal coercion. "This is a real carrot-and-stick situation," she explains. "They are facing serious prison time if they fail, but they also know that they have an opportunity to get drug treatment and help getting their lives together that would otherwise not be available."

Programs to divert drug offenders out of the criminal justice system into community treatment programs have traditionally encountered bureaucratic resistance, in large part because so many participants disappear or are quickly rearrested. Prosecutors, concerned about protecting the public safety, are reluctant to release offenders into programs where supervision is sporadic. At the same time, many treatment specialists believe that court-ordered treatment cannot "work" because it is not voluntary.

As Susan Powers observes, "The marriage between treatment and the criminal justice system can be difficult because they view offenders from very different perspectives. Treatment people see recovery as a process which includes relapse while the courts expect to enforce rules and protect the public. I think you can do both, but you have to be tough about going after those who drop out. Otherwise, no one will think the program is serious—not the offenders or the prosecutors and judges whose support is necessary to make diversion programs work."

Extensive research confirms that the threat of sanctions can be a strong incentive to stay in treatment. The longer addicts stay in treatment, the more likely they are to give up drugs and crime. A comprehensive study of the California Civil Addict program in the 1960s and 1970s, which treated drug-addicted criminal offenders, found that rates of drug use and crime among program participants were only half as great over the seven-year follow-up period compared to similar addicts not in the program.[16]

■

As communities contend with soaring corrections costs, programs which keep nonviolent drug offenders out of jail are increasingly popular. In the past decade, a number of states have opened "boot camps" where young, first-time drug offenders are sent for three to six months of "shock incarceration," involving rigorous physical exercise, work, and discipline similar to basic military training.

Despite their initial appeal as a cheaper, faster way to reform drug offenders, boot camps have not succeeded in reducing crime or drug abuse. Some, in fact, have been even less successful than traditional incarceration. In Oklahoma, for example, half the boot camp graduates returned to prison within two and a half years, compared to slightly more than one-quarter of those who had been sentenced to prison in the first place.[17]

New York State, however, uses a boot camp model which provides drug and alcohol treatment, community building, and education. It also incorporates intensive parole supervision designed to reinforce the curriculum of the shock incarceration program. In addition, the Division of Parole contracts with community-based organizations to support shock graduates following their release. Shock graduates are guaranteed a job, a place to live, and drug rehabilitation support when they return to their community. A recent twelve-month follow-up study demonstrated that less than half the shock graduates were re-arrested in the year after their release and only 11 percent were returned to prison. One-third of the boot camp beds in the United States are located in New York State.[18]

Other alternatives to incarceration range from house-arrest programs—in which offenders wear electronic bracelets to monitor their movements—to day centers—where offenders perform community service. While these programs vary widely, they usually involve weekly meetings with a supervisor, un-scheduled drug testing, and strict enforcement of probation or parole conditions. These community programs have been promoted as a way to relieve prison crowding, increase public safety, rehabilitate offenders, as well as save the taxpayer's money.

The first large-scale study of these "intensive supervision probation/parole programs," conducted by the Rand Corporation in 1990, found that they were no more effective than routine probation and parole in reducing recidivism. In some states, prison overcrowding actually increased because so many participants were incarcerated for violating parole by testing positive for drugs. And the higher costs of increased supervision meant that the programs did not save money.[19]

The most important finding of the Rand study involves drug treatment. The few programs which added intensive drug treat-ment to the mix of close supervision and drug testing reduced subsequent arrests and convictions by 10 to 20 percent. But drug treatment is so scarce that community supervision pro-grams often have great difficulty obtaining treatment for their offenders. In a Los Angeles program evaluated by the study, only 20 percent of the offenders with serious drug problems received any drug counseling. In Los Angeles County overall, fewer than 5 percent of all probationers with serious drug problems participated in drug treatment. And without treatment, intensive supervision programs are doomed to fail.

■

The most effective treatment programs view recovery as a continuing process which transforms the drug addict's life. Giving up drugs is only the first step. Gaining the personal strength and practical skills necessary to lead a productive life is often far more difficult. Most drug offenders have never possessed these skills, and very few programs provide help in acquiring them.

Delancey Street, a residential treatment program in San Francisco, teaches the most serious drug-addicted criminals everything they need to know to become model citizens. The program focuses on the entire person and his ability to function successfully in daily life rather than on his drug addiction and criminal history. To emphasize the importance of self-reliance, Delancey Street supports its operations from its own business enterprises and does not take any government funds. Its residents learn to pay their way through hard work and group effort at the same time they are working on overcoming their addiction.

Mimi Silbert, an energetic, intense woman, created Delancey Street twenty years ago after completing a Ph.D. in criminology and psychology at the University of California at Berkeley and working in the state prison system. Silbert explains that Delancey Street is really a residential educational center to bring people at the bottom of American society into the mainstream. Underlying Delancey's success, she believes, is its power to replicate the experience of a supportive, nurturing family for people who have never had it.

"At the turn of the century, Eastern European Jewish immigrants came to Delancey Street on the Lower East Side of New York," Silbert explains. "They lived in extended families and helped each other make the American dream a reality. My grandparents and parents grew up in that tradition, and we try to create that sense of family here. Most of our residents are functionally illiterate, unskilled, have been addicted for at least ten years, and have been in and out of prison four times. I have no idea what causes drug addiction, and it doesn't really matter. Whatever it is, you still have to live your life without drugs, with dignity, and make your life work for you. Delancey Street teaches people to be responsible; it is not a program for sick people who need to be taken care of."

Residents are required to earn a high school equivalency certificate; they study civics, literature, art appreciation, and music, and learn three marketable skills. The days are rigorously structured, with vocational training in one of Delancey's numerous business operations, lunchtime seminars on current events and living skills, evening educational classes, special tutoring, and group sessions. Reflecting the hierarchy of a family, more senior residents have greater responsibilities and privileges, but everyone is expected to contribute.

Delancey Street does not have paid staff. Residents teach what they have learned to newer arrivals, run the entire facility, and operate moneymaking training school businesses which include a print shop, bakery, restaurant, automotive service center, moving company, and Christmas-tree lots. "When our training schools are doing well, we all eat steak," Silbert says, "when they're not, we eat beans. But we know we're in it together for the good times and the bad."

The Delancey Street buildings, a $30 million residential and commercial complex completed in 1990, took five years to build. To get the project started, the Bank of America, which is headquartered in San Francisco, gave a $10 million unsecured loan, and local building unions provided free training. Constructed almost entirely by the residents themselves, the buildings capture the spirit of Delancey. "We didn't have $30 million, but we had faith that we could make the impossible happen," Silbert recalls. "We learned what we had to know, and in the process, our three hundred residents became expert builders. If a wall was put up badly, we tore it down and started again. We managed to complete the whole project for $14 million, and we're already paying back our bank loans."

The majority of Delancey's residents are referred by the courts; about a third walk in off the street seeking help. A screening committee of senior residents decides who can stay. Because space is limited, half the applicants are turned away. The minimum period of residence is two years, but many stay twice that long. A few have been at Delancey for eight to ten years. The dropout rate is low—about 22 percent—and half of those who leave eventually ask to return.

Silbert does not conduct follow-up studies but stays in touch with the majority of graduates. "Whether they're doing drugs or committing crimes is too narrow a measure; the more important question is whether they've changed their interaction with society," she points out. Graduates provide a network of friendship, jobs, and opportunities for each other after they leave Delancey. Some of the graduates have gone on to become stockbrokers, lawyers, real estate agents, and San Francisco city officials, including a deputy sheriff and a deputy coroner.[20]

■

At dinner time, Delancey's dining room looks like an ad for Ivy League college living, the men in ties and jackets, the women in skirts. They eat at candlelit tables set with silver and napkins, discussing the events of the day.

Karl T., a former drug addict in his early thirties, explains that learning how to relate socially is a new experience for many residents. "Out on the streets, none of us ever really talked. We shouted and fought and cursed but we didn't know how to be friendly," he remembers. Karl spent eight years at San Quentin for killing an enemy gang member, much of the time in solitary confinement. When he came to Delancey on parole, he was completely illiterate. "I had my initials tattooed over my thumb so I could copy them. Now I teach reading and writing to the new residents," he says with pride.

Mario A., who knew Karl at San Quentin, has lived at Delancey Street for three years. He has earned his high school equivalency degree and last month successfully completed his parole. When he leaves Delancey, he plans to work in an auto repair shop in Oakland owned by two Delancey graduates.

"I started using heroin when I was thirteen; my dad gave it to me," Mario recalls. "We were in the same gang; everyone did drugs, I thought it was normal. Like killing guys from other gangs. I never got caught for that, like Karl did. But I got sent up twice to San Quentin for bank robbery. I still used drugs inside. I hated the place—it made the barrio in East Los Angeles seem safe. I'd heard about Delancey Street and when my time was up, I got paroled here. This is the first real thing I've ever been in. It's like having friends and family who never quit on you, like Richard here who just would not let go, no matter how crazy I felt."

Richard P., a former cocaine dealer and drug addict who has spent five out of the past ten years in prison, laughs and puts his arm around Mario. "Man, you know we all know all the games, we can't con each other, we've all been there," Richard says. "On the street, I had friends, but only when I had money or dope. We were always waiting for someone to score. Everyone I ever trusted let me down, so I shut that part of me down. But here I found out we can be different. We're responsible for each other, so I can't run away."

"Delancey helps you grow up," Karl adds. "Whenever I've wanted to split, I look at what we've built—the walls I put up brick by brick—and the people I'm teaching who are counting on me, and I realize I can't run away."

■

Mimi Silbert is the heart and spirit of Delancey Street, which is clearly her life's work. She raised two sons there who still consider Delancey Street home. She has opened additional Delancey centers in upstate New York, New Mexico, and Santa Monica, California, with about a thousand residents nationwide.

Replicating the program without someone as dedicated and charismatic as Silbert would be difficult, but key aspects of Delancey's philosophy are more widely applicable. Delancey's emphasis on self-sufficiency, responsibility, and accountability are frequently found in effective treatment programs. So, too, are the strong group support and familylike nurturing. But Delancey also achieves practical learning in technical, educational, and social skills so that graduates have a real opportunity to build successful lives. Even seemingly small details, like learning how to choose clothes and order meals in restaurants, increase residents' confidence in their ability to function in society. The network that graduates create by opening doors for one another accelerates their progress and sustains them against the hopelessness which Silbert believes underlies drug addiction and crime.

■

We have learned in recent years that treatment of drug offenders does work. Therapeutic communities inside prisons reduce recidivism by a third to a half after inmates return to society. Special drug courts which closely monitor participation in treatment keep offenders out of jail. Contrary to popular impression, treatment does not coddle prisoners. The most effective programs are extremely rigorous, demanding far more from offenders than passive incarceration.

We know that community supervision programs for offenders on probation and parole will fail unless treatment is provided. Yet because treatment is so woefully inadequate in many cities, offenders must compete with noncriminal addicts for extremely limited space. Miami responded to this crisis by creating a treatment program solely for drug offenders referred by the court. But most courts must rely on existing treatment resources, with the result that most offenders go untreated.

The United States has the highest rate of incarceration in the world, with 1.3 million offenders behind bars. More than half these prisoners have committed drug-related crimes. Many would participate in drug treatment if it were available. Drug treatment remains our best hope for breaking the costly cycle of crime and addiction, but we have not yet begun to meet the nationwide need for new programs.

Dr. Joan Petersilia, director of Rand's Criminal Justice Program, concludes that "if Americans want real reductions in drug crime, they have to be willing to invest in programs that combine strict supervision with meaningful drug treatment. Otherwise, we are simply setting up new systems on top of old ones that just recycle the same people over and over at enormous cost."

9
■

Building
Community Coalitions

> To live with hope is to believe in the possibility of change.
> Hope is not simply willpower; we need to work together and
> find our common ground. This is the beginning of a national
> movement that can carry the day against substance abuse. This
> is the chance to mobilize the resources for a better America.
> This is a gathering of people of hope who want to repair their
> fractured communities with care and tenderness and devotion.

With this stirring invocation, the Reverend Edward Malloy,
president of the University of Notre Dame, convened the first
national meeting of community coalitions in Washington,
D.C., in November 1990. More than 450 people attended
from 172 cities.[1] This new movement had started only two
years earlier, when citizens came together in communities

across the country to create their own strategies to combat substance abuse.

Edward Foote, president of the University of Miami and chairman of the Miami Coalition for a Drug-Free Community, describes the experience of many cities in the late 1980s. "We heard the hopelessness of people in Miami—we were known as the cocaine capital of the country," he recalls. "We realized that solutions wouldn't come from Washington. Building more prisons and sending more ships to the Caribbean weren't making a difference. Instead, we needed to develop a long-term comprehensive response that involved the entire community. We knew we couldn't wait and hope someone else would do it for us. We had to take ownership of the problem."

These local antidrug coalitions harness the many different talents within a community. Volunteers from all walks of life participate directly in community action, often for the first time, and provide the impetus for many of the most creative programs. "People want to do something, but don't know what to do, so they sit around, wringing their hands. The Coalition channels this energy and helps people feel they can be part of the solution," says Marilyn Wagner Culp, executive director of the Miami Coalition, which now has more than 2,500 volunteer members. "Everyone can make a difference, by raising the level of awareness at the office, in church, in social clubs. And they can work on Coalition task forces that target specific community drug problems."

Because they are broad and diverse, community coalitions bridge the divisions that usually separate private and public, city and county drug programs. Francisca Neumann, director of Day One, Pasadena's coalition, blames bureaucratic rivalries for the weakness of earlier campaigns against alcohol and drugs. "When we put Day One together, all the different groups sat down around the table and pledged to work together. The problem was so big we realized we all had to be on the same side," Neumann says. "Day One gives us a larger perspective, so we can think as a community instead of individual programs and agencies."

The most effective antidrug coalitions draw on the strength of powerful local foundations, businesses, churches, and universities. For example, Kansas City's Metropolitan Task Force on Alcohol and Drug Abuse builds on the success of STAR, the comprehensive community prevention program which engages the city's schools, media, and civic leadership. STAR provides financial and technical support for the task force.

Gregory Dixon, deputy director of Fighting Back, the Robert Wood Johnson Foundation's nationwide initiative to encourage community coalitions, believes that STAR may be unique. "STAR is very well staffed and privately funded, and it may not be easily replicable. Most cities don't have a benefactor like Ewing M. Kauffman (founder of Marion Labs in Kansas City), who has donated millions of dollars to do remarkable things," Dixon says. "That kind of philanthropy is rare, particularly in the area of substance abuse, and it means that STAR doesn't have to rely on government bureaucracies or local fundraising for its existence."

But if STAR and other models continue to show good results, philanthropists in other cities may be willing to support additional efforts. When Eugene Lang first announced his "I Have A Dream" program in 1981, promising to pay the college tuition for all the children who graduated that year from P.S. 121 in Harlem, few believed that others would follow his lead. Yet today, there are over 150 "I Have A Dream" type projects in fifty-seven cities across the country, helping more than 12,000 children.

The Miami Coalition, one of the largest and best-organized antidrug coalitions in the country, grew out of an informal dinner meeting of business and professional leaders in April 1988. Alvah Chapman, vice chairman of the Miami Coalition and former chief executive officer of Knight-Ridder, Inc., describes the Coalition's beginnings: "Since the early 1970s, a group of forty of us have been getting together for dinner once a month to talk about what we can do to make things work better in our city. I was co-chair of this 'nongroup,' as we call ourselves, and Tad Foote kept bringing up the drug problem, but no one wanted to focus on it. Finally, I scheduled a whole evening on the subject, and we invited in drug experts and federal and city officials.

"Before the meeting, we visited treatment centers and went out with the cops on a drug sting. At our dinner, one of the enforcement officials made an impassioned plea that the problem was too big for them to handle and that the private sector had to get involved. That convinced a lot of us who were still on the fence. So I appointed a steering committee which met intensively. By the fall, we were ready to form the Coalition, name a board, and hire an executive with $1 million we raised from local corporations."

Pasadena's coalition began in March 1987 when half a dozen civic and church leaders became concerned about drug abuse resources for local youth. The group hired Francisca Neumann, who was working at the Pasadena Boys and Girls Club, to conduct a community survey which documented Pasadena's drug and alcohol problems. Using the survey as a springboard, a larger group including the mayor and key city officials decided to create a community coalition to combat substance abuse.

Day One was incorporated in 1988 with funding from Kaiser Permanente Medical Group and the City of Pasadena. Francisca Neumann explains the coalition's name as "divine inspiration." "We wanted to capture the idea that we must be anchored in the present, and work together with whatever we have to combat alcohol and drug abuse," she remembers. "Like the Alcoholics Anonymous motto that recovery is 'one day at a time,' we believe that each of us can take charge of our lives and take care of our communities beginning right now."

In the Kansas City, Miami, and Pasadena coalitions, the strong endorsement of a critical mass of local leadership—a major foundation, academic and business organizations, civic and religious groups—has been indispensable. While local government officials may play a role, these coalitions are largely volunteer efforts.

Since 1989, the Robert Wood Johnson Foundation has spent more than $50 million on its Fighting Back programs, money which is earmarked for encouraging the growth of citizen coalitions to reduce demand for drugs and alcohol. Funds have been provided to thirteen cities for five-year community prevention programs. "We are trying to stimulate comprehensive responses to alcohol and drug abuse involving prevention, treatment, and the criminal justice system which can be models for other communities," explains Gregory Dixon. "Ordinary citizens, local bureaucrats, and learned professionals are, perhaps for the first time, all on the same side when it comes to substance abuse. The toll has grown so great that many of us have set aside our differences, our biases, and our pet projects to work for the greater good of the whole society. That is the essence of Fighting Back."

Fighting Back has also stimulated the federal government to provide support for community coalitions. Since 1990, the Center for Substance Abuse Prevention (CSAP) has provided $312 million to support 252 coalitions working on substance abuse prevention, including Pasadena's Day One and the Miami Coalition.

The new coalitions have agendas that reflect the particular problems of their communities. In Gallup, New Mexico, alcoholism is rampant. Wine fortified with brandy is brought into town by tanker truckloads. A new coalition of tribal and civic leaders has taken on alcohol marketing aimed at Native Americans, and plans to deglamorize drinking through a campaign of public education and stricter enforcement of the liquor laws. In Santa Barbara, California, the Citizens' Task Force is chaired by the publisher of the local newspaper. It aims to overcome pervasive denial of substance abuse problems, which account for 80 percent of local crime, as well as educate elderly residents about the dangers of prescription drug abuse. In San Antonio, Texas, former governor Dolph Briscoe, Jr., chairs the Citizens' Task Force, which works to provide comprehensive treatment services to the city's predominantly black and Hispanic East Side, the area's major marketplace for drugs.

Because drug and alcohol abuse are closely related, most coalitions also try to change local practices which encourage drinking. In Pasadena, Day One conducted a study of alcohol-related crime to shine what Francisca Neumann calls "a flashlight in a dark place which everyone knows is a terrible problem but no one really wants to see." To try to limit public drinking, Day One members pushed successfully to prevent sales of single cold cans of beer and to convince convenience store owners that they should discourage loitering. "One way of reducing alcohol-related violence is to get people to defer their drinking until they're away from crowds of other drinkers," Neumann explains. "But we also have to create positive alternatives, so that there are well-lighted, attractive parks and recreation areas in Pasadena where abstinence is the norm."

In Kansas City, STAR works with local residents to discourage drinking and drug use, particularly among young people. In 1988 a STAR survey found that the highest levels of drinking occurred in schools located closest to convenience stores which sold beer. STAR recruited these store owners to attend its two-day "baseline" training for parents, community leaders, and other concerned citizens. The groups explore their own attitudes toward drugs and alcohol and study ways that individuals can make a contribution to substance abuse prevention in the community. After the training, the store owners agreed to enforce the drinking-age laws more rigorously. As a result, drinking in nearby schools has dropped significantly.

Cal Cormack, STAR's director, explains the theory behind this group training: "We are convinced we can draw community out of people, connect them to each other, and empower them to deal with problems like substance abuse. Once they see they can make a difference, they are usually willing to take the necessary steps, even if it means giving up something."

■

Community coalitions become advocates for changing the priorities of state and local governments, although many encounter political resistance to new initiatives. In Florida, twenty-seven community coalitions have created a statewide alliance to lobby state legislators to increase funding for prevention and treatment.

"Politicians often think about substance abuse right before elections, and then they pour more money into prisons because it looks like they're doing something," says Miami's Marilyn Culp. "Florida needs to make demand reduction a top priority instead of an afterthought, and our communities should be able to rely on dedicated funding sources, like beer taxes, to support drug treatment."

Florida's group was instrumental in getting alcohol taxes raised, but the state legislature allocated the increased proceeds to the general revenue fund rather than designating it for drug treatment. "We'll have a new strategy each year until we prevail," declares Culp. "Treatment is too important to be left to the whims of the political process."

In Washington, D.C., the Corporation Against Drug Abuse (CADA) was created in late 1988 by a group of the city's professional, corporate, and civic leadership. CADA's first step was to commission independent studies to assess Washington's substance abuse problems and devise effective strategies to address them.[2] CADA found that Washington schools do not have comprehensive drug prevention programs but rely on general health curricula, while nearby Maryland and Virginia schools use a number of different prevention programs. CADA concluded that effective community prevention programs were urgently needed and that Kansas City's STAR should be introduced into all junior high schools in the greater metropolitan area. Thus far, however, progress has been slow. STAR is currently operating in only fifteen schools in the District of Columbia.

"The sad thing is that our public schools will not embrace prevention," says Connie Bush, CADA's community prevention program director. "The research is right there on STAR's results. The Kauffman Foundation provided the initial training, which CADA is now supporting. But systems don't like change. Principals and teachers see this as one more thing they have to do, even though it means our kids are missing out." CADA hopes to extend STAR to additional schools in Washington. The coalition will continue to campaign for comprehensive community prevention programs in all area junior high schools.

Coalitions are often able to appeal effectively for community support for a wide range of new programs. In northwest Pasadena, Sheila Clark, a counselor at the Jackie Robinson Community Center, works with pregnant drug abusers in nearby public housing projects, urging them to seek treatment. She immediately ran into a roadblock: the only residential program in the area refused to provide space for the women's children. Clark brought the issue to Day One, and Francisca Neumann persuaded the Junior League to support a new center where women could stay with their children. "Day One has mustered the support of the entire city," Clark observes. "Fran hooks up different places and people to get things done."

Three thousand miles away, the Miami Coalition also helps generate political support for new approaches, like the Dade County Drug Court which diverts first-time drug offenders from the criminal justice system into closely supervised treatment. "Without the Coalition, we would never have been able to get all the different agencies to agree to the Drug Court," says Judge Herbert Klein. "It takes real clout to overcome ingrained bureaucratic resistance to new ways of operating, and the Drug Court looks revolutionary!" In order to finance the $1.3 million annual cost of the new program, Chief Judge Gerald Wetherington raised Miami traffic-school fees by $10 and negotiated successfully with the county government to direct the majority of the additional revenues to the Drug Court.[3]

■

Getting drugs out of the workplace is a central focus for many coalitions, reflecting business concerns about employee absenteeism, productivity, safety, and higher health insurance rates. The Miami Coalition's Business Against Narcotics and Drugs (BAND) has recruited 500 companies, which employ half the local workforce, to set up model drug programs. BAND has also published a drug policy manual in Spanish as well as English for small businesses.

In Washington, D.C., CADA offers free assistance to employers to help them establish drug-free programs and is working with small businesses to develop affordable employee assistance programs. In Pasadena, Day One cooperates with the local Chamber of Commerce to convince local businesses that they will save money and improve performance by adopting strong antidrug policies. It also publishes a manual of prevention and treatment resources within Pasadena and holds four seminars a year to educate employers on how to reduce drug abuse in the workplace.

Coalitions often enlist local media to expand community awareness of drug and alcohol problems as well as to build public support for their efforts. Newspaper publishers, advertising agencies, and heads of TV and radio stations are valuable coalition members, who can arrange for contributions of free radio, television, and print media spots. Some coalitions have been particularly successful. The Miami Coalition, which enlisted media involvement at the outset, raised over $3.5 million in donated air time and print space in its first year. In 1989 BAND carried out an intensive two-month media campaign to let Miami residents know that "We're banding together—the business community against narcotics and drugs," and giving out a telephone number to call to join the effort. Within a year, the number of companies participating in BAND jumped from 55 to 276.

The Coalition has also used the media to enlist direct public participation in making sure that drugs are not sold near schools, effectively turning the larger community into citizen patrols. "Very few people knew about our 1987 law prohibiting drugs within one thousand feet of a school," Marilyn Culp recalls. "So we got the PTA to post big signs inside all the schools warning that drugs were off-limits, and the Chamber of Commerce to put up similar signs outside. Then we did media spots educating people about the law and asking anyone who saw any suspicious activity near a school to call a special police number. The police let the schools know if an arrest is made so the schools can track the case through the courts."

■

Today coalitions are making a major difference in many cities, bring more informed, better-funded strategies to bear on local drug problems. As T. Willard Fair, director of Miami's Urban League, points out, "The Coalition lifted the issue of drug abuse to a point of urgency in the larger community, and made many people aware that they have responsibilities. When the power brokers of the community bring together corporate resources to bear on the problem, clearly you're going to get some changes." Surveys conducted in 1993 by independent Miami researchers indicate the Coalition is making progress—many citizens believe the drug problem is getting better and report fewer cases of drug abuse in schools and workplaces.

The deep concern many Americans feel about substance abuse is a powerful catalyst for community action. Coalitions are channeling that concern into programs that require active citizen participation, connecting people to each other and their communities in entirely new ways. These efforts generate enormous human energy, as coalition members discover that they can make a difference, even against seemingly intractable problems like substance abuse. This sense of empowerment is critically important in overcoming the hopelessness and apathy that often prevent communities from taking action.

The coalitions, like all volunteer initiatives, depend on the commitment of their members as well as on the leadership of a few highly dedicated individuals. Sustaining that commitment over time is a difficult challenge. Many coalitions have responded by creating small professional staffs to share the administrative burden. But the uniqueness of these efforts lies in their ability to engage many different parts of the community in a common campaign to drive out drugs, led largely by volunteers who care deeply about the future of their cities.

James Burke, chairman of the Partnership for a Drug Free America, believes the coalitions are providing vital new answers to America's drug problems: "We elect people to go solve our problems, but the federal government can't and won't solve this one. The people who know how to are those who are closest to it—parents, police, teachers, local businessmen, and media. This is old-fashioned democracy at work, where communities forge their own solutions."

10

$\blacksquare$

Changing Public Attitudes

The media may be the single most powerful force that shapes American attitudes about acceptable behavior. Young people are particularly susceptible; the vast majority of teenagers spend an average of six hours a day listening to radio and watching television. In recent years, intensive advertising campaigns have strengthened negative attitudes toward illegal drugs, reinforcing school and community prevention efforts.[1]

In 1987 the Partnership for a Drug Free America launched the largest public service advertising campaign in the nation's history. A volunteer coalition of advertising, media, and public communications firms, the Partnership set out to "unsell" illegal drugs.

The goal is total market saturation, explains James Burke, chairman of the Partnership and former CEO of Johnson & Johnson: "We have set out to raise $1 million a day in contributed air time and print space, which means that virtually every American will see an antidrug message every day." So far, the Partnership has generated more than $1.7 billion in donated creative and production services, television and radio airtime, and print space. By the end of 1993, 17,000 antidrug Partnership TV spots had been aired, almost half during network prime time, while Partnership ads appeared in more than 1,300 daily newspapers and 200 magazines. Antidrug ads are also displayed in bus shelters, before feature films in theaters, in previews on commercial rental videos, and in shop-at-home catalogues.[2]

The Partnership campaign, which draws on the same marketing techniques used to promote commercial products, is far more sophisticated than earlier efforts. In the past, antidrug public service announcements were low-budget productions, rarely shown in prime time. They often featured well-known sports or entertainment stars who had recovered from drug abuse. Subsequent studies have questioned the effectiveness of these commercials because they conveyed the ambiguous message that a drug abuser can still succeed phenomenally in life. The ads did not "deglamorize" drugs or drug users.[3]

The Partnership approaches the marketing of its ideas very differently. Its ads encourage hostility toward marijuana, cocaine, and crack, and make drug use look pathetic, unattractive, and foolish. Before new material is aired, it is thoroughly tested to make sure the message is getting through to the target audience.

Key to this process are focus groups which the Partnership holds in communities across the country. A typical session in an elementary school in Flushing, New York, recently reviewed anticrack ads aimed at preteens. Five fourth-grade students, who had been selected by their teacher to participate in the focus group, attentively watched three one-minute spots. A graphic depiction of a young man being bitten by a snake while smoking crack emerged as the group's favorite. One nine-year-old boy suggested that the ad would be better if the young man died, so that youngsters would know that "using drugs is throwing your life away." Another pointed out that the ad would remind kids that smoking crack was dumb, like playing with poisonous snakes. The children's reactions were later used to refine the final version of the television spots.

Allen Rosenshine, the head of BBDO Worldwide, one of the world's largest advertising agencies, chairs the Partnership's monthly creative reviews of new advertising. He sees the ads as extraordinary opportunities to change public behavior. "The challenge is to reach adults and kids who don't think drugs are a problem for them," Rosenshine explains. "We have to give people a reason to think about the issue again. Simply telling them drugs are bad won't do it, because they already know that. We need to make them respond in a way they wouldn't have before. Each commercial has to be targeted like a rifle shot —so that in a few seconds, it gives everyone who's watching an attitude and a habit of resistance toward drugs."

Many of the Partnership ads are dramatic portrayals of the serious risks of illegal drug use. A print ad entitled "Cocaine" shows a teenage boy holding a revolver up his nose; another depicts the now familiar image of a single egg frying on a stove under the caption, "This is your brain on drugs." A television spot called "Pool Party" shows an unsuspecting girl diving into an empty swimming pool, while the voice-over warns, "Before you go and do something you've never done before, you'd just better know what you're jumping into."

Advertising is carefully tailored to take into account the developmental realities of the target audience. As the most effective school prevention programs have demonstrated, young teenagers are much more influenced by the need to fit in socially than by abstract warnings of the dangers of drug use. A

television spot aimed at marijuana smoking shows a boy looking admiringly at a girl across a room at a crowded party. As he
approaches her, she lights up a joint, and he turns away in
disgust. The message is clear—drug use is unattractive and
results in social isolation, the worst fear of most adolescents.

Some Partnership ads suggest how concerned citizens can
take action against drugs. Those directed at employers, for
example, portray employees using drugs at work and carry the
recommendation, "Make him choose between getting treatment and getting fired." The ads often provide the number of
the NIDA Helpline, which was established in 1987 to provide
advice on how to organize a drug-free workplace. In 1991 the
Helpline received more than one thousand calls a month from
private employers and labor unions in response to Partnership
advertising.

Recent ads try to engage parents in drug prevention. Caroline Jones, who runs her own advertising agency in New York
City, has developed several spots directed at black families as
part of the Partnership's effort to reach minority groups. Jones
believes that "procrastination by parents is one of the great
enemies of kids. Our ads ask parents to make appointments
with their kids to sit down and talk. The message is simple:
find the time to talk to your kids about drugs before there is no
time." The ads also explain how to obtain a free copy of the
Parents' Guide to Prevention, prepared by the U.S. Department
of Education to help parents discuss drugs with their children.
More than 12 million guides have been requested through an
800 telephone number.

Annual tracking studies on the effects of the Partnership
campaign have found substantial changes in both attitudes and
drug use.[4] Children ages nine to twelve who watch Partnership
ads on a regular basis have become the most antidrug group
in America. The number of children who have friends who

"sometimes use" marijuana has dropped almost by half since 1987. At the same time, children report talking to their parents and teachers much more about drugs than in the past.

Where Partnership ads are seen most frequently, improvement is greatest. In Miami and Minneapolis, where the ads run often, changes in attitude are two to three times larger than in Chicago and Los Angeles, where donated air and print space has been smaller.

Partnership chairman James Burke believes that the nation is "turning off drugs" because of a profound cultural shift. "Americans are deciding in record numbers that using illegal drugs is no longer acceptable behavior," Burke says. "And they are beginning to recognize that the drug problem is embedded in every other serious social problem in America today. We have to find a solution to illegal drug use if we are going to alleviate society's other social ills, and I believe the public realizes this."

∎

Until very recently, American businesses have often been reluctant to be associated with highly visible antidrug efforts, in part because they fear the public will assume that their employees have drug problems. An exception is Members Only, a manufacturer of casual men's clothes, one of the few companies to sponsor a major advertising campaign using only antidrug messages. The $25 million effort, which lasted from 1986 to 1990, graphically portrayed the consequences of drug addiction and violence. Commercials were hard-hitting, like one which showed a police badge being riddled with bullets and then told viewers, "Drugs don't just kill drug addicts." Although the company's name appeared in the commercials, its clothing did not. Instead they urged young people, who are the main buyers of Members Only clothes, to join the battle against drugs.

During the campaign, Members Only's sales increased 25 percent and the company acquired a reputation for being both "hip" and caring. Ruth Wooden, president of the Advertising Council, believes that the Members Only campaign "amplified the message that drug abuse has an impact on corporations and helped create a greater discussion about what companies can do."[5]

■

Media campaigns also play an important role at the local level both in changing public attitudes and in recruiting greater support for community antidrug efforts. In Orange County, California, the citizens' coalition has mobilized the media to take aim at drug users. Sheriff Brad Gates, the moving force behind the Orange County campaign, recounts how the jump in local cocaine deaths in late 1986 changed his thinking. "We stepped up our efforts against major dealers, but that wasn't making any difference. We were arresting more people and putting them behind bars, but the problem wasn't getting any better. Then we realized that we needed a complete attitude change about drugs. There aren't any laws against tobacco and it's available everywhere, but people still quit smoking. We believe that when you inform people about the dangers, the great American spirit will take over. Media is the way to do it."

Working with the Orange County coalition, Disneyland created three new cartoon characters—Skippy, Spike, and Wise Owl Mike—to teach elementary school children "the right way to act around drugs." A cartoon booklet, *Free from Drugs —A Lifetime Script to Follow,* leads children and their parents through basic information about alcohol, tobacco, and drugs and provides games and exercises to test refusal skills. The booklet has been distributed to schools throughout Orange County.

In addition, the Orange County coalition was active in convincing Disney and other major studios to produce a half-hour antidrug cartoon special entitled "All Stars to the Rescue," featuring dozens of the most popular cartoon figures—Donald Duck, Mickey Mouse, Winnie the Pooh, the Ninja Turtles, Miss Piggy, and Kermit the Frog, among others. Underwritten by the Ronald McDonald Foundation, the program was aired simultaneously on all three major television networks on April 21, 1990, to an estimated audience of 32 million viewers. Since then, 350,000 videotapes and family viewer educational materials have been distributed free to schools and community groups nationwide. Roy Disney, the show's executive producer, says, "If we can capture the attention and imaginations of young people for just a minute, and leave a lasting impression, we will have accomplished our goal."

■

Media efforts to discourage smoking and drinking are still very limited. The Partnership's antidrug campaign does not include tobacco and alcohol, in large part because many of its supporting organizations also benefit from the $6 billion the alcohol and tobacco industry spend annually on promotion.

Although there are no television commercials currently running nationally that point out the dangers of alcohol and tobacco use, other approaches are being tried. The Center for Health Communication of the Harvard School of Public Health launched a campaign against drinking and driving in December 1987. Working with television writers and producers, the project has succeeded in having dialogue introduced into the scripts of popular programs to reinforce the norm that the driver does not drink. On *L.A. Law*, for example, the Christmas episodes in 1990 and 1991 made repeated references to the need for designated drivers in connection with holiday parties. In addition, the three major television networks have produced and sponsored prime-time public service announcements promoting the designated-driver concept, with particularly heavy coverage during the holidays. Tracking data collected by the Gallup Organization in 1990 found that more than two-thirds of adults who go to parties where alcohol is served had recently seen a designated-driver ad and that the use of designated drivers had increased significantly.[6]

"Entertainment not only mirrors social reality, but also helps shape it by depicting popular opinion and by influencing people's perceptions of appropriate behavior," explains Dr. Jay Winsten, the Center's director. "The strength of using 'no driving after drinking' dialogue in popular programs is that short messages embedded within the story, presented by characters who serve as role models within a dramatic context, facilitate social learning." No-drinking messages for minors have also been incorporated in television programs. For example, *Full House* and *Family Matters,* two popular family situation comedies, each recently devoted a thirty-minute episode to the problem of underage drinking.

■

It is because television and radio advertising are such powerful forces in shaping behavior that tobacco and alcohol commercials (except for wine and beer) have been banned from the air. The average American teenager sees 2,500 beer and wine commercials on television every year.[7] And the tobacco companies direct a substantial portion of their print advertising toward youngsters, even though sales to minors are illegal. A recent study of RJR-Nabisco's "Old Joe Camel" campaign found that six-year-old children recognize Old Joe Camel as easily as Mickey Mouse. Since the campaign began in 1988, Camel's share of the illegal children's market has jumped to one-third compared to the brand's less than 9 percent share of the adult market. Camel's sales to minors represent $476 million a year. It is not surprising that tobacco use among the young is increasing, after remaining steady for the past decade.[8]

The impact of antismoking television ads in the late 1960s is instructive. From 1967 to 1971, when cigarette ads were banned, broadcasters were required to donate airtime to counter commercial cigarette advertising. Antismoking messages received a total of $200 million in donated airtime—at that point the largest media campaign ever waged against smoking. Adult per capita smoking declined by more than 10 percent, the first time that consumption had fallen for more than two consecutive years. When the anticigarette ads ended in 1971, smoking immediately resumed its upward trend.[9]

Eighteen years later, California launched the largest offensive yet undertaken against smoking. Supported by revenues from higher cigarette taxes, the program spends $80 million a year for advertising, educational campaigns in schools, and programs by local health and community organizations. Thousands of antismoking ads attack the tobacco industry as merchants of death on television, radio, and highway billboards. During Saturday morning cartoons, special ads tell preteens they're smarter than their parents because they don't smoke. Ads tailored to minority communities, which are subject to especially heavy tobacco promotion, show black and Hispanic men giving up cigarettes and saying they don't find women who smoke attractive.

In the three years since the antismoking campaign began, smoking among California adults has dropped 17 percent. If current trends continue, the percentage of Californians who smoke is expected to decline to 6 percent by the year 2000, compared to 26 percent in 1987. In a statewide survey, more than three-quarters of those interviewed identified the antitobacco ads, and substantially larger numbers of smokers reported that they intended to quit after seeing them. Although the higher cigarette tax of twenty-five cents a pack also discourages smoking, California's intensive educational and advertising campaign is clearly strengthening negative attitudes toward tobacco.[10] Smoking is declining in California much more rapidly than in the rest of the country. In 1992, 26 percent of all Americans age twelve and over were current smokers, a decline of only 6 percent since 1985.[11]

■

Given the power of alcohol and tobacco advertising, it is encouraging that drinking and smoking are declining at all. What progress we have made is largely attributable to growing public awareness of health dangers both to the user and to others. The threat of harm from passive smoking or from drivers who have been drinking has greatly strengthened negative social attitudes toward tobacco and alcohol. The annual Surgeon General's Report on smoking has had a major impact on public perceptions, and health warnings on tobacco products and in advertisements also help. Two-thirds of Americans believe that smoking a pack of cigarettes a day is very hazardous.[12] While requirements for warning labels on alcoholic beverages adopted in 1991 are narrower than those on tobacco products (warning of adverse effects on the fetus and impairment of the capacity to operate heavy machinery and automobiles), they, too, have begun to send a larger social message about alcohol. In 1992, 65 percent of Americans aged twelve and over reported drinking in the previous year, compared to 73 percent in 1985.[13]

The illegality of marijuana, heroin, and cocaine conveys a strong message that these drugs are harmful and that society disapproves of their use. The fact that role models from all walks of life—athletes, musicians, movie stars, community and church leaders—now speak out against drugs also reinforces negative attitudes. As these attitudes become more widespread in our society, they create an environment that actively discourages drug use. National surveys report that one-fifth of youngsters aged twelve to seventeen have tried illegal drugs compared to more than half who have tried drinking or smoking—clear evidence that drugs are much less socially acceptable. But powerful as they are, antidrug attitudes are not enough to prevent drug use. Without solid educational and employment opportunities, many people have no hope for the future. For them, drug use provides instant escape, and drug dealing offers immediate income, despite the risks of injury and arrest. Creating real alternatives for those whose circumstances make them most vulnerable to drugs is crucial if we are to build on the progress we have already made in changing public attitudes toward drugs.

12
.

Toward a Drug-Free America

The despair that "nothing works," which I heard from the midwestern newspaper publisher and many others around the country as they first tried to grapple with the crack epidemic, was understandable. But we have made enormous progress in recent years. We now know that there are new strategies that give us reason to hope.

Effective drug prevention programs *can* reduce the likelihood that children—even those at highest risk—will use drugs and alcohol. New approaches to treatment *can* help addicts stay off drugs and keep offenders out of jail. Neighborhoods and local police working together *can* drive dealers off the streets. Companies *can* create comprehensive drug programs which reduce drug use among their employees. Business, media, and civic leaders *can* forge powerful antidrug coalitions which transform communities.

Yet many Americans still despair that nothing works. They may not know about these encouraging new initiatives, which have not yet received concentrated national attention. Or they may not believe that they work. The new antidrug strategies reflect a very different vision of how to combat substance abuse, rejecting the traditional view that America's drug problems can best be solved by reducing supplies through tougher law enforcement and interdiction. The new vision focuses instead on reducing demand, changing attitudes, and engaging citizen participation.

Many Americans still think of drugs as an external threat to the nation's well-being, and political leaders reinforce this notion. For example, President Bush explained that the U.S. invasion of Panama in 1989 was necessary to curtail General Manuel Noriega's drug trafficking, and called for increased resources to combat "narcogangsters": "They must be dealt with by our military in the air, on the land, and on the seas." Since then, the military has greatly increased its role in drug interdiction. "When the Cold War ended, the Defense Department suddenly realized the drug war was one they could love," explains a senior drug policy official in Washington. "They could reclassify some of their existing programs and still get new funding. They just turned the radars watching for cruise missiles over Canada south to look for drug traffickers."

But none of this has made a difference. Since Noriega's capture, cocaine shipments through Panama have increased substantially. Greater military involvement in interdiction has not reduced the volume of drugs coming into America—nor has it made our streets safer, reduced the dangers that face our children, or restored the many lives shattered by drugs.[1]

Contrary to assumptions we have held for almost a century, other countries are not to blame for this very American disease, even if many foreigners earn huge profits from it. The market is fueled by American appetites, not foreign drug lords. And, as we have seen with marijuana, LSD, and the "designer" drugs, American producers are fully capable of supplying American demand.

■

We are in the midst of the largest war on drugs in our history, a war that gives unprecedented importance to enforcement and interdiction. Yet drug crime continues to rise. At the same time, many Americans are turning away from marijuana and cocaine, in large part because they believe these drugs are harmful. What we see emerging is an increasingly divided nation—in which the greatest declines in drug use are occurring among the better educated and affluent while addiction is growing among the poor and disadvantaged.[2] As this divide deepens, there is a real danger that law enforcement will become an even more dominant part of the nation's response.

Record antidrug expenditures—which in 1993 alone cost federal, state, and local governments over $40 billion—have not bought victory. We now have the highest rate of addiction in our history, exceeding even that at the turn of the century, when opiates, cocaine, and marijuana were legally marketed. We also have the highest rate of imprisonment in the world, largely because of drug-related crime.

We do not need a bigger drug war which pours even more resources into trying to seal the nation's borders, eradicate foreign drug crops, and lock up addicts. We need an entirely different approach built on what we have learned about reducing drug abuse and drug crime. The most promising strategies are coming not from Washington, but from communities working to find new solutions to their drug problems. They are moved by the simple, but critically important discovery that the answers to America's drug problem lie here at home. They recognize that no one can escape the myriad effects of drug abuse on our families and society, and that they must therefore "take ownership" of this problem.

This recognition is central to many of the most effective antidrug initiatives, bringing new energy to a problem which often has seemed too large and complex for ordinary citizens to address. In inner-city neighborhoods, courageous organizers like Washington, D.C.'s Doris Watkins and Pasadena's Audrey Brantley have reclaimed their streets from drug dealers and forged new relationships with law enforcement officials. In Detroit's Pilgrim Village, "taking ownership" for REACH's Charlene Johnson has literally meant renovating dilapidated crack houses and selling them to local families who work to improve the neighborhood. Community coalitions are encouraging citizen participation in new antidrug strategies which produce visible results. The nationwide media campaign led by the Partnership for a Drug Free America has strengthened the belief that individuals—whether as parents, employers, teachers, or in other roles—have the responsibility and the power to take action against drug abuse.

This new vision can lead to transformations at the local level, like the success of Kansas City's STAR in persuading convenience-store owners not to sell alcohol to high school students, as well as on a larger political level, like Florida's statewide organization of community coalitions which is lobbying in Tallahassee to increase state spending for demand-reduction programs.

We have learned that substantial progress can be made even on a small scale—within a neighborhood, a family, a school, a prison. We do not have to wait until we know how to attack the "root causes" of addiction and crime—the complex individual, familial, and environmental factors that contribute to these problems—or be able to support massive programs of social reconstruction. There is much that can be done immediately to reduce drug addiction and its harmful effects.

Drug addiction both creates and intensifies other serious problems, such as homelessness, child abuse, violent crime, and AIDS. A 1991 Rand study of intensive probation and parole programs confirmed what many experts have long believed—that drug abuse has become so pervasive that unless it is directly addressed, even the best-designed social programs will fail. Although jailing drug offenders may be successful in keeping them off the streets, there is very little chance that punishment alone will prevent them from committing new crimes after their release. Within three years, almost half will be arrested again, continuing the costly cycle of addiction, crime, and violence.[3] In much the same way, efforts to slow the spread of AIDS will fail unless they recognize the central importance of drug abuse in transmitting the virus. Getting addicts to stop using dirty needles will require expanding treatment, including methadone maintenance, as well as providing clean needles.

Attacking drug abuse even when it is deeply intertwined with many other serious problems can produce good results. Drug prevention programs which have traditionally targeted school children also hold promise for the most disadvantaged youngsters who are not in school. As the Strengthening Families program has shown, effective prevention helps children of drug abusers reduce their alcohol and tobacco use and improve their behavior, even if their parents continue to use drugs. Abused and neglected children who participate in the Westchester Student Assistance Program in several New York State residential facilities also show improvement. Even without addressing the complex range of problems these children face, substantial progress is possible in helping them deal with substance abuse, which may in turn improve other aspects of their lives.

■

The most promising prevention, education, and treatment programs share certain common features. They all explicitly recognize the realities of substance abuse and its devastating impact on individuals, families, and communities. Breaking through the silence of denial opens up the possibility of change—in suburban high schools, impoverished inner cities, and corporate boardrooms. Bank Street's Project Healthy Choices helps very young children talk about the substance abuse they see around them as the first step in teaching them how to make healthy choices in their own lives. The Westchester Student Assistance Program essentially does the same thing with teenagers from far more privileged homes. Major corporations which have developed successful antidrug programs, such as Capital Cities/ABC, have first had to face the fact that their employees were not immune to drug abuse.

In treatment, too, overcoming denial is the critical first step to recovery. The most successful programs help addicts come to that recognition as quickly as possible. As New York Hospital's Dr. Robert Millman points out, "Most drug abusers start out believing that they can successfully manage their drug use so that it does not get out of control. Even when their lives are falling apart, they still may not recognize that they have a serious problem because they think they are special, invulnerable." At therapeutic communities, such as Phoenix House, encounter groups help residents break through denial and see that their experiences are not unique. At Alcoholics Anonymous and Narcotics Anonymous meetings, acknowledging the power of addiction over the individual is central to recovery.

The newest approaches to prevention also recognize the realities of substance abuse. We have learned that scare tactics do not deter youngsters. Teaching children the immediate effects of drinking, smoking, and trying drugs has proved far more effective than exaggerated threats of their dangers. At the same time, programs like LST and STAR attack the widespread adolescent belief that "everyone is doing it." Understanding that use is far more limited than most youngsters imagine helps them resist pressures to use drugs to gain acceptance among their peers.

Effective programs share another common feature—they teach people how to make healthy life choices which do not include drugs. The first step is learning that there are choices, even in very difficult situations where substance abuse is pervasive. In Boys and Girls Clubs in public housing projects as well as STAR classrooms in junior high schools, youngsters talk about the good and bad things that might happen if they accept a marijuana joint from an older friend. Their teachers push them to think through the consequences and test them out on each other, so that they fully understand their choices. As Bank Street's Healthy Choices shows us, children have to play with ideas before they are able to make them part of their own thinking. This approach is far more complex—and effective—than simply repeating a slogan like "just say no," which may be quickly forgotten in the face of real pressure to drink, smoke, and use drugs.

The most successful programs provide practical skills which help translate the desire to live without drugs into reality. Life Skills Training, for example, teaches twelve- and thirteen-year-olds how to resist social pressure and to make decisions that will help them achieve their goals. Even if children want to refuse offers of drugs, they need to know what to say and how to act without being rejected by their peers. Having the opportunity to practice these skills with each other in the safety of the classroom gives them confidence which will help them in more threatening situations.

Even very young children, like the four- and five-year-olds participating in Strengthening Families, benefit from learning how to get help from adults such as teachers and neighbors, and how to deal with their parents more effectively. At Delancey Street, criminal offenders with long histories of drug addiction learn basic social skills which are essential to their success. "Good vocational programs often fail because their graduates don't know how to handle normal social interactions and fly off the handle if their boss criticizes their work," Mimi Silbert explains. "At Delancey, we try to build up the 'social capital' of our residents—teaching them how to control their anger, talk politely with each other, handle responsibility, dress appropriately, and even order from a restaurant menu—so that they feel comfortable in mainstream society. Otherwise they will always think of themselves as outcasts and act that way."

The most effective approaches to reducing drug abuse break through the individual isolation and social fragmentation which feed hopelessness. Interaction is the key to prevention, for both very young children who are just learning to talk about their daily experiences and teenagers who are already drinking and trying drugs. In treatment, too, overcoming the isolation of addiction is critically important, whether through the fellowship of AA meetings, counseling and group therapy, or friendships with other recovering addicts.

"Bringing the community out in people so they connect to each other helps them see ways that they can personally prevent drug abuse," explains Kansas City's Cal Cormack. This experience also animates communities which are fighting back against drugs and crime. Neighborhood organizers like Miami's T. Willard Fair and Pasadena's Audrey Brantley have found new allies within the police force, city agencies, and civic leadership in their efforts to reclaim their streets from drug dealers. On a larger level, community coalitions are overcoming fragmentation, bringing much-needed leadership to the assault on drugs.

Good programs are even stronger if they can offer powerful alternatives to drug use. Amity's Naya Arbiter thinks of these alternatives as "a toolbox of new ideas, skills, opportunities, and friendships which replace the drugs which have dominated the addict's life." Recovering addicts frequently describe the delight of "waking up to life." It is not surprising that recovery rates are generally twice as high among addicts who have families, jobs, and friends. The pain of addiction soon outweighs its pleasures, and most addicts, even those with fewer personal supports, want to get rid of the "monkey" on their back. But educational and job opportunities clearly accelerate recovery. Miami's Drug Court offers vocational training and help finding jobs for drug offenders who stick with the intensive treatment program. By 1992, only one in four participants had dropped out or been rearrested, and 91 percent of the program's graduates had found full-time employment.

In prevention efforts, too, providing attractive alternatives to substance abuse is critically important. Drinking and drug use are the major forms of recreation in many neighborhoods, in the inner city as well as the wealthy suburbs. Youngsters often do not know how to enjoy themselves in any other way. Drug-free dances and sporting and social events provide social alternatives, which also strengthen teenagers' resistance to drugs and alcohol. Safe, supervised recreation can make a difference even in the most disadvantaged areas, as we have learned from the sharp reductions in cocaine use and vandalism within housing projects which have Boys and Girls Clubs.

Creating an environment that rejects drug use and dealing is fundamental to these promising new antidrug strategies. Social attitudes are immensely powerful in influencing individual behavior, as we see from the recent declines in marijuana and cocaine use among better-educated Americans. The Partnership for a Drug Free America is successfully "unselling" drugs and increasing public disapproval of drug use. Corporate America has reinforced the no-use message in the workplace with antidrug policies, drug testing, and employee assistance programs.

The power of social attitudes to shape behavior has also been demonstrated at the local level by programs like Kansas City's STAR, which engages families, schools, the media, and community leaders. Even within a classroom, changing students' views of alcohol, tobacco, and drugs creates a more hostile environment, which discourages them from using. Establishing new norms that rule out drug use is especially important in prisons, where separate therapeutic communities are often the only drug-free zones which support the recovery of addicted offenders.

■

While reducing the demand for drugs offers the best hope for real progress, it does not happen overnight. Anyone who has struggled to give up smoking or lose weight knows that changing behavior is a continuing process which needs constant reinforcement. The most effective classroom drug-prevention programs are stronger if their lessons are amplified at every level of influence—in the family, the media, the community —and if booster lessons are given as children move through adolescence.

Treatment, too, is a continuing process rather than a single episode from which the addict emerges cured. Although the initial phase requires intensive participation—whether in therapeutic communities such as Amity or highly structured non-residential programs such as Matrix—successful recovery usually involves an extended period of after-care, learning to function effectively without drugs with the help of other recovering addicts, friends, and family. Relapse is part of the recovery process for drug addicts, as it is for smokers and alcoholics, but at least one in three addicts eventually succeeds. With intensive treatment, strong support, and job and educational opportunities, the recovery rate is much higher.

We have learned that law enforcement plays an important role, but it should not be the centerpiece of drug policy. While street sweeps can clear out drug dealers, these gains disappear without the active involvement of neighborhood residents. As Doris Watkins discovered in Washington, D.C.'s Marshall Heights, it is impossible to drive out drug dealing—even with police support—unless the residents themselves refuse to tolerate it. As police move beyond their traditional role, they are working with communities to make neighborhoods safer and more able to resist crime. Better street lighting, more frequent trash pickups, and park maintenance can discourage dealers from coming back. Civil code enforcement is a powerful tool in driving dealers from dilapidated buildings and holding landlords responsible. In disadvantaged neighborhoods like northwest Pasadena and Detroit's Pilgrim Village, these efforts have sharply reduced drug crime and violence.

The limits of law enforcement have become painfully clear in the past decade.[4] Drug arrests nationwide have increased by half while the prison and jail population has more than doubled. Faced with continuing increases in drug addiction and crime, many Americans still believe that the only solution is even larger expenditures for police, courts, and prisons. But the rapid buildup in enforcement in recent years has already greatly increased punishment without any measurable improvement in crime rates. Washington, D.C., leads the nation's cities in arrests and convictions of drug dealers and users, and street dealers face a one-in-five chance of going to jail in any single year. Yet even these odds have not dented the crime rate, since more than three-quarters of Washington's dealers are supporting drug habits from their earnings.[5] Without treatment, they will continue dealing undeterred by the threat of punishment.

Treatment under court supervision, however, can make a substantial difference, as we have seen in the new drug courts in Miami and Oakland and the Brooklyn district attorney's Drug Treatment Alternative to Prison program. What distinguishes these efforts from traditional diversion programs is that treatment is provided immediately after arrest rather than several months later (or in many cities, not at all) and participants know with certainty that they will be returned to jail for dropping out. Legal coercion can be a powerful incentive to change but only if it is accompanied by meaningful treatment which makes change possible.

■

Drug, alcohol, and tobacco abuse costs our country $237 billion a year, according to a 1993 Brandeis University study. This estimate includes costs related to illness, deaths, productivity losses, and crime. Of the total cost, illicit drug abuse accounted for $67 billion. The cost of keeping 1.35 million Americans behind bars, for example, is nearly $25 billion a year; at least half this amount is attributable to drug crime.[6] The enormity of these costs dwarfs the annual federal antidrug budget, which in 1994 stands at approximately $13 billion. Pointing out this wide discrepancy, many politicians call for even more funds to fight our nation's drug war.

But the politicians are wrong. What we need is not more

money but an entirely different strategy, one that puts into practice what we have learned in recent years about reducing the demand for drugs. Many of the most promising new approaches are not expensive compared to the costs of prison construction and sophisticated high-tech equipment intended to seal the nation's borders against the drug traffic.

Two of the most effective school prevention programs, LST and STAR, cost about $15 to $25 per pupil, including classroom materials and teacher training. They reduce new smoking and marijuana use by half and drinking by one-third and these results are sustained for at least three years.

Intensive drug-treatment programs within prisons, such as Stay'n Out and Cornerstone, cost $4,000 to $8,000 a year for each inmate. Rearrest rates among graduates after they are released from prison are cut by one-third to one-half.

Oakland's "speedy diversion program," which immediately puts drug offenders into treatment under close court supervision, costs $800,000 a year. In the program's first year, rearrests of drug offenders dropped by half.[7]

The Miami Coalition, which has a small professional staff and relies largely on volunteers, has a yearly budget of $200,000 yet it has leveraged $6.2 million in new community resources to fight substance abuse.

Programs like these, which give us reason to hope that we can make a lasting impact on America's drug problem, are still isolated examples of success. They are often developed by inspired individuals, like Delancey Street's Mimi Silbert and Miami's T. Willard Fair, or dedicated researchers, like LST's Gil Botvin and Strengthening Families's Karol Kumpfer, who do not have the resources to market their ideas to the larger public. In some cities, antidrug coalitions have taken the lead in reaching out to find more about what works to put into practice in their own communities. But more often, overbur-dened local officials, faced with shrinking resources and no reliable guidance, make choices which do not reflect the best of what we know.

We know that a drug-free America is within our grasp. We know that drug abuse is largely driven by demand, not supply, and we have learned how to reduce demand successfully. Over the past decade, we have developed the tools to build a strategy that will make a lasting impact. Now is the time to start.

dependence, a withdrawal syndrome—which can include irritability, depression, and insomnia—is reported following abrupt cessation of use.

LYSERGIC ACID DIETHYLAMIDE (LSD)

First synthesized in 1938 in Switzerland, LSD is the most potent of the hallucinogens. It is supplied by illicit manufacturers within the United States.

LSD triggers perceptual and thought changes, which vary widely depending on the individual, situation, and dosage. Users report that colors seem brighter, shapes are distorted, and boundaries shift and dissolve. LSD increases blood pressure and body temperature and accelerates heart and reflex rate. LSD can produce feelings of great insight as well as anxiety, depression, and acute panic, which sometime lead to accidents or destructive behavior during "bad trips." LSD is not physically addictive, although its effects are highly unpredictable.

PHENCYCLIDINE (PCP)

Developed in the late 1950s as an anesthetic in veterinary medicine, PCP was taken off the market in the late 1970s because of widespread abuse. However, the drug continues to be produced illicitly from easily obtained chemicals.

PCP is probably the most unpredictable of all psychoactive drugs. Its effects include euphoria, numbness, reduced inhibitions, paranoia, hallucinations, and delusions. In high doses, PCP can cause convulsions, coma, and death. PCP's effects are intensified by alcohol and depressants, increasing the risk of overdose. Like LSD, PCP can cause "bad trips," which recur later through flashbacks.

RESOURCES FOR FURTHER INFORMATION

1. THE SUPPLY-SIDE SEDUCTION

National Institute on Drug Abuse (NIDA)
    5600 Fishers Lane
    Rockville, MD 20857
    (301) 443-1124/5

National Institute of Alcohol Abuse and Alcoholism
(NIAAA)
    Willco Building, Suite 409
    6000 Executive Boulevard
    Rockville, MD 20892-7003
    (301) 443-3860

Center for Substance Abuse Prevention (CSAP)
    5600 Fishers Lane, Suite 800
    Rockwall II Building
    Rockville, MD 20857
    (301) 443-0373

To obtain free NIDA, NIAAA, and CSAP publications, including the *National Household Survey on Drug Abuse and Drug Use Among American High School Seniors, College Students and Young Adults,* and booklets on creating drug-free communities, call:

National Clearinghouse for Alcohol and Drug Information (NCADI)
    11426 Rockville Pike
    Suite 200
    Rockville, MD 20852
    (800) 729-6686
    Contact: Information Specialist Director, ext. 470

For additional information regarding the national survey of high school seniors, college students, and young adults, contact:

Institute for Social Research
    Room 2311
    The University of Michigan
    Ann Arbor, MI 48106-1248
    (313) 763-5043

Office of National Drug Control Policy
    The Executive Office of the President
    Washington, DC 20500
    (202) 395-6700

For reports of the United States General Accounting Office, contact:

U.S. General Accounting Office
P.O. Box 6015
Gaithersburg, MD 20884-6015
(202) 512-6000

The Sentencing Project
   918 F Street, N.W.
   Suite 501
   Washington, DC 20004
   (202) 628-0871

National Head Start Association
   201 North Union Street
   Suite 320
   Alexandria, VA 22314
   (703) 739-0875

Institute on Black Chemical Abuse
   2614 Nicollet Avenue South
   Minneapolis, MN 55408
   (612) 871-7878

Drugs and Crime Data Center and Clearinghouse
   1600 Research Boulevard
   Rockville, MD 20850
   (800) 666-3332

2. DRUGS IN THE AMERICAN MIND

Advocacy Institute (tobacco and alcohol issues)
   1730 Rhode Island Avenue, N.W.
   Suite 600
   Washington, DC 20036-3118
   (202) 659-8475

Children of Alcoholics Foundation, Inc.
   P.O. Box 4185
   Grand Central Station
   New York, NY 10163-4185
   (212) 754-0656

Center for the Future of Children
  The David and Lucille Packard Foundation
  300 Second Street
  Suite 102
  Los Altos, CA 94022
  (415) 948-3696

March of Dimes Birth Defects Foundation
  Greater New York Chapter
  233 Park Avenue South
  New York, NY 10003
  (212) 353-8353

Parent Resources Institute on Drug Education (PRIDE)
  10 Park Place South, Suite 304
  Atlanta, GA 30303
  (404) 577-4500

3. TEACHING PREVENTION

Project STAR (Students Taught Awareness and Resistance)
  Youth Development
  Ewing Marion Kauffmann Foundation
  4900 Oak Street
  Kansas City, MO 64112
  (816) 932-1000

Project Healthy Choices
  Bank Street College of Education
  610 West 112th Street
  New York, NY 10025
  (212) 875-4510

Institute for Prevention Research
  The New York Hospital–Cornell University
  Medical College
  411 East 69th Street, Room 201
  New York, NY 10021
  (212) 746-1270
  Contact: Gilbert J. Botvin, director

Center for Prevention Research
  University of Kentucky
  1151 Red Mile Road
  Suite 1-A
  Lexington, KY 40504
  (606) 257-5588

4. HELPING HIGH-RISK KIDS

For information on the Westchester Student Assistance Program, contact:

Student Assistance Services Corporation
  300 Farm Road
  Ardsley, NY 10502
  (914) 674-0400
  Contact: Ellen Morehouse

SMART Moves
  Boys and Girls Clubs of America
  771 First Avenue
  New York, NY 10017
  (212) 351-5468
  Contact: Gale Barrett-Kavanagh

Safe Haven Project
  Department of Health
  Keifer Health Complex
  Bureau of Substance Abuse
  1151 Taylor, Building 1
  Detroit, MI 48202
  (810) 647-7463
  Contact: Georgia Aktan, principal investigator

Strengthening Families Program
  Department of Health Education
  HPERN-215
  University of Utah
  Salt Lake City, UT 84112
  (801) 581-7718
  Contact: Karol Kumpfer

Social Development Research Group
  School of Social Work
  University of Washington
  146 North Canal Street
  Suite 211
  Seattle, WA 98103
  (206) 543-6742

5. DEALING WITH DEALERS

Police Foundation
  1001 22nd Street, N.W., Suite 200
  Washington, DC 20037
  (202) 833-1460

The Vera Institute of Justice
  377 Broadway
  New York, NY 10013
  (212) 334-1300
  Contact: Mike Farrell for information on the Community
  Policing Program

Citizens Committee for New York City, Inc.
  305 Seventh Avenue, 15th Floor
  New York, NY 10001
  (212) 989-0909
  Contact: Olga Moya

Program in Criminal Justice Policy and Management
  Harvard University
  John F. Kennedy School of Government
  79 John F. Kennedy Street
  Cambridge, MA 02138
  (617) 495-5188

American Alliance for Rights & Responsibilities
  1725 K Street, N.W.
  Suite 1112
  Washington, DC 20006
  (202) 785-7844

6. DRIVING DRUGS FROM THE WORKPLACE

Legal Action Center
  153 Waverly Place
  New York, NY 10014
  (212) 243-1313

Office of National Drug Control Policy
  Executive Office of the President
  Washington, DC 20500
  (202) 467-9660

National Institute on Drug Abuse (NIDA)
  Office of Workplace Initiatives
  Parklawn Building
  5600 Fishers Lane
  Rockville, MD 20857

  Center for Substance Abuse Prevention Workplace Helpline
  (800) 843-4971

7. TREATING ADDICTION

The Matrix Center
  9033 Wilshire Boulevard
  Suite 201
  Beverly Hills, CA 90211
  (213) 655-4518

Drug Abuse Research Center
  UCLA
  1100 Glendon
  Suite 763
  Los Angeles, CA 90024
  (310) 825-9057

Midtown Center for Treatment and Research
  55 West 44th Street
  2nd Floor
  New York, NY 10036
  (212) 764-5178
  Contact: Carl Castagna, director
           Roger Camber, medical director

Phoenix House Foundation
  Office of Public Information
  164 West 74th Street
  New York, NY 10023
  (212) 595-5810

Al-Anon Family Group, Inc.
  Box 862, Midtown Station
  New York, NY 10018-0862
  (800) 344-2666

Alcoholics Anonymous
  General Service Office
  Box 459, Grand Central Station
  New York, NY 10163
  (212) 870-3400

Amity
  P.O. Box 32200
  Tucson, AZ 85751-2200
  (602) 749-7201

Therapeutic Communities of America
  1818 N Street, N.W.
  Suite 300
  Washington, DC 20036
  (202) 296-3503

For information on methadone programs, contact:

New York State Office of Alcoholism and Substance
Abuse Services
  Licensing Services
  55 West 125th Street
  New York, NY 10027
  (212) 961-8464

8. TREATING CRIMINAL OFFENDERS

NDRI (Narcotic & Drug Research, Inc.)
11 Beach Street
New York, NY 10013
(212) 966-8700

NCCD (National Council on Crime and Delinquency)
685 Market Street
Suite 620
San Francisco, CA 94105
(415) 896-6223

Rand Criminal Justice Program
1700 Main Street
P.O. Box 2138
Santa Monica, CA 90401
(310) 393-0411 ext. 6321

Delancey Street Foundation
600 Embarcadero
San Francisco, CA 94107
(415) 957-9800

For information on the Miami Drug Court, contact:

Metro-Dade Office of Substance Abuse Control
111 N.W. First Street
Suite 2740
Miami, FL 33128
(305) 375-2676

For information on the Oakland drug court and the recently formed Coalition of Drug Court Jurisdictions, contact:

The Hon. Jeffrey S. Tauber
  661 Washington Street
  Oakland, CA 94607
  (510) 268-7606

DTAP (Drug Treatment Alternative to Prison Program of the Brooklyn District Attorney)
  Municipal Building
  210 Joralemon Street
  Brooklyn, NY 11201
  (718) 802-2072
  Contact: Susan A. Powers, deputy district attorney

9. BUILDING COMMUNITY COALITIONS

Fighting Back
  National Program Office
  2553 The Vanderbilt Clinic
  Nashville, TN 37232-5305
  (615) 343-9603

Day One
  132 North Euclid Avenue
  Pasadena, CA 91101
  (818) 796-1172
  Contact: Francisca Neumann

REACH, Inc.
  1840 Midland
  Detroit, MI 48238
  (313) 345-8727

Miami Coalition for a Safe and Drug Free Community
400 S.E. Second Avenue
4th Floor
Miami, FL 33131
(305) 375-8032

CADA (Corporation Against Drug Abuse)
Community Prevention Program
3917 Minnesota Avenue, N.E.
Washington, DC 20019
(202) 397-7300
Contact: Constance H. Bush

10. CHANGING PUBLIC ATTITUDES

The Media-Advertising Partnership for a Drug Free America, Inc.
405 Lexington Avenue, 16th Floor
New York, NY 10174
(212) 922-1560

For information on the Harvard Alcohol Project, contact:

Center for Health Communication
Harvard School of Public Health
677 Huntington Avenue
Kresge Building 3
Room 334
Boston, MA 02115
(617) 432-1038

OTHER RESOURCES

For a copy of the *Citizen's Alcohol and Other Drug Prevention Directory: Resources for Getting Involved*, call NCADI, (800) 729-6686.

For a copy of *State Drug Resources: A National Directory*, call the Drugs & Crime Data Center & Clearinghouse, (800) 666-3332.

NOTES

INTRODUCTION

1. C. Peter Rydell and Susan S. Everingham, *Controlling Cocaine: Supply vs. Demand Programs* (Santa Monica, Calif.: RAND Corporation, 1994), p. xviii.

1. THE SUPPLY-SIDE SEDUCTION

1. Information on alcohol, tobacco, and illicit drug use comes from the *National Household Survey on Drug Abuse 1992* (Rockville, Md.: National Institute of Drug Abuse, 1993). The survey, which is now conducted annually, is based on interviews of Americans age twelve and older who are living in households. Since it does not include people who are transient, homeless, or in jails or other institutions, the survey probably underestimates drug use among certain groups. The survey (hereafter cited as *Household Survey 1992*) appears in two volumes, *Main Findings* and *Population Estimates*. Not all data from the survey are published each year. Previous surveys are cited as *Household Survey 1990* and *Household Survey 1991*.

2. For estimates of treatment needs as well as an encyclopedic review of treatment research, see Dean R. Gerstein and Hendrick J. Harwood, eds., *Treating Drug Problems: A Study of the Evolution, Effectiveness, and Financing of Public and Private Drug Treatment Systems,* Institute of Medicine (Washington, D.C.: National Academy Press, 1990); hereafter cited as *IOM Study.*

3. Seven in ten Americans see drug abuse as a greater problem now compared to five years ago, and fully half see it as a much greater problem than in the past. Forty percent of Americans indicate that the problem has forced them to change the way they live, by making their homes more secure, staying inside at night, and avoiding certain areas. Peter D. Hart Research Associates, Inc., *American Attitudes Toward the Drug Problem and Drug Policy,* Study no. 3942, February 1994.

4. See Arnold M. Washton, *Cocaine Addiction: Treatment, Recovery, and Relapse Prevention* (New York: W. W. Norton, 1989).

5. Charlotte B. McCullough, "The Child Welfare Response," *The Future of Children* (Center for the Future of Children, The David and Lucile Packard Foundation), vol. 1, no. 1 (Spring 1991), 63.

6. Estimates of drug-exposed infants born in the United States each year vary widely. The National Association for Perinatal Addiction Research reports that one out of ten newborns—about 375,000—is exposed in the womb to illicit drugs, and in the major cities the number is 20 percent or higher (Anastasia Toufexis, "Innocent Victims," *Time,* May 13, 1991, 57). Deanna S. Gomby and Patricia H. Shiono ("Estimating the Number of Substance-Exposed Infants," *The Future of Children,* vol. 1, no. 1 [Spring 1991], 17–25) estimate that 158,000 infants are exposed to cocaine each year, and between 554,400 and 739,200 pregnant women use one or more illegal drugs. The *IOM Study,* using substantially lower estimates of maternal drug use, calculates that 105,000 pregnant women annually need drug treatment. See also *Drug Abuse: The Crack Cocaine Epidemic: Health Consequences and Treatment,* GAO/HRD-91-55FS (Washington, D.C.: General Accounting Office, January 1991).

7. For statistics on violent crime, see Kathleen Maguire, Ann L. Pastore, and Timothy J. Flanagan, eds., *Sourcebook of Criminal Justice*

Statistics 1992, U.S. Department of Justice, Bureau of Justice Statistics (Washington, D.C.: Government Printing Office, 1993), 357; hereafter cited as *Crime Sourcebook.*

8. National Institute of Justice, *Drug Use Forecasting 1992 Annual Report* (Washington, D.C.: Department of Justice, 1993).

9. "Some Administration officials say they are bracing for a new wave of heroin addiction, with heroin possibly replacing crack as the drug of choice in urban ghettoes by the end of the decade." (Clifford Krauss, "U.S. Reports Gains in Drug War, But the Battles Keep on Shifting," *New York Times*, July 14, 1991). See also *National Drug Control Strategy: Reclaiming Our Communities from Drugs and Violence* (Washington, D.C.: Office of National Drug Control Policy, 1994); hereafter cited as *National Drug Control Strategy 1994*. In April 1994, the Drug Abuse Warning Network (DAWN) reported increases in heroin-related overdose cases and emergency-room mentions between 1992 and 1993.

10. Mathea Falco, "Beating the Next Drug Crisis," *World Monitor*, February 1990, 46.

11. For a brief review of federal drug policy from 1968 to 1988, see Mathea Falco, *Winning the Drug War: A National Strategy* (New York: Priority Press Publications, Twentieth Century Fund, 1989). President Richard Nixon allocated two-thirds of the federal antidrug budget to treatment and prevention, which declined to slightly more than one-half under Presidents Gerald Ford and Jimmy Carter. Higher heroin prices resulting from deep cuts in Turkish and Mexican opium production in the 1970s, though short-lived, forced some addicts into treatment. The government's reliance on treatment as its major weapon against drug abuse continued until 1981, when President Reagan radically shifted spending priorities away from demand reduction toward drug law enforcement.

12. My estimate is based on a Rand Corporation calculation of total drug enforcement expenditures for 1989, which found that state and local governments spent slightly more than twice as much as the federal government. Federal drug enforcement spending from 1981 to 1993 amounted to about $47 billion. Assuming the Rand ratio provides a reasonable measure, total federal, state, and local drug enforcement spending for the period would have exceeded $130 billion.

13. For evaluation of air interdiction efforts between 1982 and 1989, see *Drug Smuggling: Capabilities for Interdicting Private Aircraft Are Limited and Costly*, GAO/GGD-89-93 (Washington, D.C.: General Accounting Office, June 1989). The chances of airborne smugglers getting caught are negligible. In 1990 the U.S. military spotted 6,729 suspicious flights, but law enforcement succeeded in seizing only 49 aircraft (*Drug Control: Impact of DOD's Detection and Monitoring on Cocaine Flow*, GAO/NSIAD-91-297 [Washington, D.C.: General Accounting Office, 1991]). See also *Counter-Drug Congressional Justification FY95*, Department of Defense, 1994.

14. For an excellent discussion of illicit drug production, see Peter Andreas, Eva Bertram, Moris Blachman, and Kenneth Sharpe, "Dead-End Drug Wars," *Foreign Policy*, no. 85 (Winter 1991–92), 106–28. Estimates come from Peter Reuter, Gordon Crawford, and Jonathan Cave, *Sealing the Borders: The Effects of Increased Military Participation in Drug Interdiction* (Santa Monica, Calif.: Rand Corporation, 1988), 123, and Leslie Gelb, "Yet Another Summit," *New York Times*, November 3, 1991.

15. See Reuter, Crawford, and Cave, *Sealing the Borders*.

16. Philip Shenon, "The Score on Drugs: It Depends on How You See the Figures," *New York Times*, April 22, 1990.

17. The *IOM Study* reports that private hospitals and clinics provide only one-quarter of the nation's treatment capacity, even though they receive 40 percent of America's total treatment spending. Of the 5.5 million Americans who the IOM estimates need drug treatment, as many as 4.2 million must rely on public programs. Only 600,000 publicly funded treatment "slots" are currently available.

18. See Fox Butterfield, "U.S. Expands Its Lead in the Rate of Imprisonment," *New York Times*, February 11, 1992. The Sentencing Project in Washington, D.C., which compiles current estimates of the total prison and jail population, places the average cost of incarcerating one inmate at more than $18,000 a year. See *Crime Sourcebook* for information on drug-related crime.

19. Office of AIDS Surveillance, New York City Health Department, 1994. See also *The Effectiveness of Drug Abuse Treatment: Impli-*

cations for Controlling AIDS/HIV Infection, Background Paper on OTA's Series on AIDS-Related Issues, no. 6 (Washington, D.C.: Office of Technology Assessment, U.S. Congress, September 1990), 31, 33; and Don Des Jarlais et al., "HIV-1 Infection Among Intravenous Drug Users in Manhattan, New York City, from 1977 Through 1987," *Journal of the American Medical Association,* vol. 261 (1989), 1008.

20. In 1988, 21.1 million Americans aged twelve and older acknowledged using marijuana in the previous year, compared to 17.4 million in 1992. During the same period, 8.2 million Americans reported "past year" cocaine use, compared to 4.9 million in 1992. (*Household Surveys 1988* and *1992*). Denise Kandel concludes that "attitudes appear to be the crucial proximal determinant of drug use, as has been demonstrated for cigarette smoking," in "The Social Demography of Drug Use," *Milbank Quarterly* (1991). For a thorough discussion of the challenges of estimating drug-use prevalence, see Peter Reuter, "Prevalence Estimation and Policy Formation," *Journal of Drug Issues,* vol. 23, no. 2 (Spring 1993), 167–84.

21. Data on drug use among children, teenagers, and young adults are drawn largely from Lloyd D. Johnston, Patrick M. O'Malley, and Jerald G. Bachman, *Drug Use Among American High School Seniors, College Students, and Young Adults, 1975–1992* (Rockville, Md.: National Institute on Drug Abuse, 1993); hereafter cited as *Johnston Survey 1992.* The Institute for Social Research, University of Michigan, conducts the survey annually. When possible, I have used 1993 data from a University of Michigan press release dated January 31, 1994; hereafter cited as *Johnston Survey 1993.*

22. *Household Survey 1991.* Gordon S. Black Corporation, *The Attitudinal Basis of Drug Abuse: The Third Year,* prepared for the Partnership for a Drug Free America (Rochester, N.Y.: September 19, 1989).

23. *Household Survey 1990.*

24. In 1992, 24 percent of college-bound seniors had used drugs, compared to 34 percent of those not planning to continue their education (*Johnston Survey 1992,* vol. 1, 110).

25. *National Drug Control Strategy 1994.* See also *The President's Drug Strategy: Two Years Later—Is It Working?* prepared by the Majority Staffs of the Senate Judiciary Committee and the International Narcotics Control Caucus (Washington, D.C.: September 1991), 73.

26. *Household Survey 1992.* In 1992, 642,000 Americans aged twelve and older used cocaine at least once a week, compared to 662,000 in 1990. In 1992, 26.4 percent of young adults aged eighteen to twenty-five reported using illegal drugs at least once in the past year, compared to 28.7 percent in 1990 and 32 percent in 1988. Among young adults reporting illegal drug use at least once a month, the same pattern is evident: In 1992, 13 percent reported monthly drug use, compared to 14.9 percent in 1990, and 17.8 percent in 1988. (The *Household Survey* was not conducted in 1989.) Hospital emergency-room statistics are reported quarterly by the Drug Abuse Warning Network (DAWN), National Institute of Drug Abuse, Rockville, Md.

27. *Crime Sourcebook 1992,* tables 4.9, 5.16.

2. Drugs in the American Mind

1. This section is drawn from three classics on the history of American drug control: David T. Courtwright, *Dark Paradise: Opiate Addiction in America Before 1940* (Cambridge: Harvard University Press, 1982); David Courtwright, Herman Joseph, and Don Des Jarlais, *Addicts Who Survived: An Oral History of Narcotic Use in America, 1923–1965* (Knoxville: University of Tennessee Press, 1989); and David F. Musto, *The American Disease: Origins of Narcotic Control,* expanded edition (New York: Oxford University Press, 1987). A good, brief historical overview is provided by David Musto in "Opium, Cocaine, and Marijuana in American History," *Scientific American,* July 1991, 40–47.

2. Holmes quote is taken from Peter T. White, "Coca–An Ancient Indian Herb Turns Deadly," *National Geographic,* January 1989, 32.

3. Courtwright, *Dark Paradise,* 78. For further reading on the history of cocaine, see Patricia G. Erickson, *The Steel Drug: Cocaine in Perspective* (Cambridge: Harvard University Press, 1982); Lester

Grinspoon and James B. Bakalar, *Cocaine: A Drug and Its Social Evolution* (New York: Basic Books, 1975); and Joseph Spillane, "Some Preliminary Observations on the History of Cocaine," Rand Corporation, Draft Report, May 29, 1991.

4. Courtwright, *Dark Paradise*, 97.

5. Musto, *The American Disease*, 282, note 15.

6. The narcotics clinics, like other public health facilities which treated tuberculosis, syphilis, and mental illness, generally served the poor. Few clinics claimed many cures, but most tried to stabilize their clients' lives by giving them regular doses of narcotics. Some clinics also attempted to reduce drug-related crime, which was stimulated by the high prices charged for narcotic prescriptions by some private doctors and pharmacies. In New Haven, the Police Department ran the clinic. Addicts were registered at City Hall and given drugs at low cost under the supervision of police doctors and pharmacists.

7. Musto, *The American Disease*, 220.

8. National Commission on Marihuana and Drug Abuse, *Marihuana, A Signal of Misunderstanding*, vol. 2, Washington, D.C., 1972. Two excellent sources for the changing social consensus toward drug use and American drug policy during the 1960s are Edward M. Brecher and the editors of Consumer Reports, *Licit and Illicit Drugs* (Mount Vernon, N.Y.: Consumers Union, 1972); and Patricia M. Wald and Peter B. Hutt, *Dealing with Drug Abuse* (New York: Praeger, 1972).

9. *Johnston Survey 1993.*

10. *Crime Sourcebook* (see chapter 1, note 7), table 2.87.

11. Institute for Health Policy, Brandeis University, *Substance Abuse: The Nation's Number One Health Problem* (Princeton, N.J.: Robert Wood Johnson Foundation, October 1993). For a comprehensive review of data on the prevalence and costs of alcohol, tobacco, and illegal drug use as well as a thoughtful analysis of the contrasting approaches to legal and illegal drugs, see Steven Jonas, "The U.S. Drug Problem and the U.S. Drug Culture: A Public Health Solution," in James A. Inciardi, ed., *The Drug Legalization Debate*, Studies in Crime, Law and Justice, vol. 7 (Newbury Park,

Calif.: Sage Publications, 1991); Steven Jonas, "Solving the Drug Problem: A Public Health Approach to the Reduction of the Use and Abuse of Both Legal and Illegal Recreational Drugs," *Hofstra Law Review*, vol. 18, no. 3 (Spring 1990), 751–93; and Steven Jonas, "The Public Health Approach to the Prevention of Substance Abuse," in Joyce Lowinson, Pedro Ruiz, and Robert Millman, eds., *Comprehensive Textbook of Substance Abuse* (Baltimore, Md.: Williams and Wilkins, 1992).

12. For a fascinating account of the decline in smoking since the Surgeon General's Report in 1964, see Kenneth E. Warner, "The Effects of Publicity and Policy on Smoking and Health," *Business and Health*, November 1984, 7–13.

13. In "Addictive Drugs: The Cigarette Experience" (unpublished paper prepared for the Rand Drug Policy Research Center, 1991), the economist Thomas C. Schelling points out that the success rate for smokers achieving at least two years' abstinence is one in five or one in six per attempt. He notes that the eventual success rate for quitting is one in two, but only because of repeated efforts.

14. *Children of Alcoholics: Facts* (New York: Children of Alcoholics Foundation, 1992). According to Deanna S. Gomby and Patricia H. Shiono ("Estimating the Number of Substance-Exposed Infants," *The Future of Children*, vol. 1, no. 1 [Spring 1991], 17–25), "the incidence of fetal alcohol syndrome . . . is approximately 1.9 births per thousand. . . . We estimate that as many as 73 percent of pregnant twelve- to thirty-four-year-olds may have drunk alcohol sometime during their pregnancies." See also George Steinmetz, "The Preventable Tragedy: Fetal Alcohol Syndrome," *National Geographic*, February 1992, 36–39.

15. For discussion of adverse effects on infants of maternal cocaine use, see Lisa Zeitel, Tamar Bauer, and Phyllis Brooks, *Infants at Risk: Solutions Within Our Reach* (New York: Greater New York March of Dimes/United Hospital Fund of New York, 1991), 34. See also Ira Chasnoff, "Drug Use in Pregnancy: Parameters of Risk," *The Pediatric Clinics of North America*, vol. 35, no. 6 (December 1988), 1403–12; and Ira Chasnoff, "Temporal Patterns of Cocaine Use in Pregnancy: Perinatal Morbidity and Mortality," *Journal of the American Medical*

Association, vol. 261 (1989), 1741–22. For a straightforward summary of this research, see *Drug-Exposed Infants—A Generation at Risk*, GAO/HRD-90-138 (Washington, D.C.: General Accounting Office, June 28, 1990).

More recent medical commentary suggests that poverty, community violence, inadequate education, and diminishing employment opportunities may also account for the developmental difficulties of drug-exposed infants, and warns that "condemning these children with labels of permanent handicap and failure is premature and may lead us to overlook what we have long known about the remediating effects of early intervention." See Linda Mayes, Richard Granger, Marc Bornstein, and Barry Zuckerman, "The Problem of Prenatal Cocaine Exposure: A Rush to Judgment," *Journal of the American Medical Association*, vol. 267 (1992), 407.

16. *The President's Drug Strategy: Two Years Later—Is It Working?*, prepared by the Majority Staffs of the Senate Judiciary Committee and the International Narcotics Control Caucus (Washington, D.C.: September 1991), 87. For a comprehensive discussion of recent research on maternal substance abuse and an overview of prevention, treatment, and public policy, see *Pregnancy and Substance Abuse: Perspectives and Directions*, Symposium proceedings, *Bulletin of the New York Academy of Medicine*, 67 (May-June 1991).

17. Zeitel, Bauer, and Brooks, *Infants at Risk*.

18. *The Public Health Impact of Needle Exchange Programs in the United States and Abroad*, School of Public Health, University of California, Berkeley, and the Institute for Health Policy Studies, University of California, San Francisco (October 1993). *The Effectiveness of Drug Abuse Treatment: Implications for Controlling AIDS/HIV Infection*, Background Paper on OTA's Series on AIDS-Related Issues, no. 6 (Washington, D.C.: Office of Technology Assessment, U.S. Congress, September 1990), 110.

19. *IOM Study*, 1990, 142–46. See also *Effectiveness of Drug Abuse Treatment*, 71, which summarizes outcomes of properly run methadone maintenance programs: "The proportion of methadone maintenance clients abstaining from heroin [for more than two years] was 85 to 98 percent. Overall, 2-year retention rates exceeded 65 percent

. . . reduction in cocaine use (30 to 40 percent decline) and alcohol abuse (30 to 40 percent decline) . . . more than a 70-percent decline in criminal acts and arrests reported in some programs."

20. Estimates of the numbers of heroin addicts generally range from 500,000 to 700,000 (see *IOM Study* and Peter Reuter, "Prevalence Estimation and Policy Formation," *Journal of Drug Issues*, vol. 23, no. 2 [Spring 1993], 167–84). Approximately 95,000 clients were participating in methadone maintenance programs as of September 30, 1989. See U.S. Department of Health and Human Services, *Highlights from the 1989 National Drug and Alcoholism Treatment Unit Survey* (NDATUS) (Rockville, Md., July 1990). Using the most conservative estimate, methadone treatment is available for fewer than 20 percent of the nation's heroin addicts.

3. TEACHING PREVENTION

1. *Household Survey 1992* reported that 448,000 American youths aged twelve to seventeen used marijuana, 24,000 used cocaine, and 858,000 used alcohol at least once a week. For a detailed analysis of risk factors which contribute to adolescent substance abuse, pregnancy, delinquency, and school failure, see Joy G. Dryfoos, *Adolescents at Risk: Prevalence and Prevention* (New York: Oxford University Press, 1991).

2. A Gallup poll conducted in January 1990 reported that 40 percent of American adults think drug education should be the government's first priority, while 28 percent support working with foreign governments to curtail drug supplies. Only 19 percent think arresting dealers is the most promising strategy. See Mary H. Cooper, "Does the War on Drugs Need a New Strategy?" *Editorial Research Reports*, vol. 1, no. 8 (February 23, 1990), 118.

3. Nancy J. Kaufman, "Smoking and Young Women: The Physician's Role in Stopping an Equal Opportunity Killer," *Journal of the American Medical Association*, February 23, 1994, 629–30.

4. For a thorough review of earlier school prevention programs, see Phyllis L. Ellickson, "School-Based Drug Prevention: What Should It Do? What Has to Be Done?" in Robert Coombs and Douglas

Ziedonis, eds., *Handbook of Drug Abuse Prevention* (Boston: Allyn and Bacon, 1994). See also Gilbert J. Botvin, "Substance Abuse Prevention: Theory, Practice, and Effectiveness," in Michael Tonry and James Q. Wilson, eds., *Drugs and Crime* (Chicago: University of Chicago Press, 1990), 461–519.

5. U.S. Congress, Office of Technology Assessment, *Adolescent Health—Volume II: Background and the Effectiveness of Selected Prevention and Treatment Services*, OTA-H-466 (Washington, D.C.: Government Printing Office, November 1991), 536–45, provides a thorough review of recent prevention research.

6. Numerous studies link the marketing of women's cigarette brands with the prevalence of smoking among women and girls. See John P. Pierce, Lora Lee, and Elizabeth A. Gilpin, "Smoking Initiation by Adolescent Girls, 1944 Through 1988: An Association with Targeted Advertising," *Journal of the American Medical Association,* February 23, 1994, 608–11.

7. *Household Survey 1991* (see chapter 1, note 1).

8. Gilbert Botvin, Eli Baker, Linda Dusenbury, et al., "Preventing Adolescent Drug Abuse Through a Multimodal Cognitive-Behavioral Approach: Results of a 3-Year Study," *Journal of Consulting and Clinical Psychology,* vol. 58, no. 4 (1990), 437–46. See also Gilbert Botvin and Linda Dusenbury, "Substance Abuse Prevention and the Promotion of Competence," in L. A. Bond and B. E. Compas, eds., *Primary Prevention and Promotion in the Schools* (Newbury Park, Calif.: Sage Publications, 1989).

9. Mary Ann Pentz, J. H. Dwyer, D. P. Mackinnon, et al., "A Multicommunity Trial for Primary Prevention of Adolescent Drug Abuse," *Journal of the American Medical Association,* vol. 261 (1989), 3259–66. See also Mary Ann Pentz, E. A. Trebow, William B. Hansen, et al., "Effects of Program Implementation on Adolescent Drug Use Behavior: The Midwestern Prevention Project (MPP)," *Evaluation Review,* vol. 14 (1990), 264–89.

10. Dr. Mary Ann Pentz, personal communication, January 11, 1992.

11. C. Anderson Johnson, Mary Ann Pentz, Mark Weber, et al., "Relative Effectiveness of Comprehensive Community Programming for Drug Abuse Prevention with High-Risk and Low-Risk Adolescents," *Journal of Consulting and Clinical Psychology,* vol. 58, no. 4 (1990), 447–56.

12. Data on youngsters aged twelve to seventeen are drawn from *Household Survey 1992,* 85. Data on high school seniors are from *Johnston Survey 1993* (see chapter 1, note 21).

13. Joel M. Moskowitz, "The Primary Prevention of Alcohol Problems: A Critical Review of the Research Literature," *Journal of Studies on Alcohol,* vol. 50, no. 1 (1989), 54–88. See also Diana Chapman Walsh and Lynn Elinson, "Effectiveness of Measures to Prevent Alcohol-Related Problems: An Update," unpublished paper (Geneva: World Health Organization, January 1992).

14. Richard Clayton, Anne Cattarello, and Katherine Walden, "Sensation Seeking as a Potential Mediating Variable for School-Based Prevention Intervention: A Two-Year Follow-Up of DARE," *Health Communication,* vol. 3, no. 4 (1991), 229–39; and Richard Clayton, Anne Cattarello, L. Edward Day, and Katherine Walden, "Persuasive Communication and Drug Prevention: An Evaluation of the DARE Program," in Lewis Donohew, Howard Sypher, and William Bukoski, *Persuasive Communication and Drug Abuse Prevention* (Hillsdale, N.J.: Lawrence Erlbaum Associates, 1991). See also Christopher Ringwalt, Susan Ennett, Kathleen Hold, "An Outcome Evaluation of Project DARE," in *What Do We Know About School-Based Prevention Strategies?* Papers for a conference at the University of California, San Diego (UCSD Extension, October 18–19, 1990). This compendium of previously published and unpublished work from leading prevention researchers is a useful reference.

· 15. R. Bangert-Drowns, "Effects of School-Based Substance Abuse Education—A Meta-Analysis," *Journal of Drug Education,* vol. 18 (1988), 243–64.

16. *National Drug Control Strategy 1994,* 5. For 1995, President Clinton has requested $660 million for school drug prevention programs,

an increase of $191 million. Even a doubling of funds will be ineffective, however, unless schools know which programs are effective.

17. William B. Hansen, "School-Based Substance Abuse Prevention: A Review of the State of the Art in Curriculum, 1980–1990," *Health Education Research*, vol. 7, no. 3 (1992), 403–30, provides an extraordinarily thorough analysis of the relative effectiveness of school prevention programs.

18. Judith Fagin and Ruth Sauer, *Evaluation Report: Project Healthy Choices* (New York: Special Consulting Services, Inc., 1990).

4. Helping High-Risk Kids

1. Joy G. Dryfoos, *Adolescents at Risk: Prevalence and Prevention* (New York: Oxford University Press, 1991). See also David A. Hamburg, *Today's Children: Creating a Future for a Generation in Crisis* (New York: Times Books, 1992) for a comprehensive, compassionate discussion of the needs of developing children.

2. For an eloquent summary of risk-factor research and its implications for policy, see J. David Hawkins, "Risk-Focused Prevention: Prospects and Strategies," Presentation to the Federal Coordinating Council on Juvenile Justice and Delinquency Prevention (June 23, 1989). See also Barry S. Brown and Arnold R. Mills, eds., *Youth at High Risk for Substance Abuse* (Rockville, Md.: National Institute on Drug Abuse, 1987).

3. *Johnston Survey 1993.*

4. These studies can be obtained from Ellen R. Morehouse, Westchester Student Assistance Program, 300 Farm Road, Ardsley, N.Y. 10502. See also John D. Swisher, Stanley B. Baker, James A. Barnes, et al., "An Evaluation of Student Assistance Programs in Pennsylvania," Pennsylvania State University Department of Counselor Education, Counseling Psychology, and Rehabilitation Services Education, December 1990.

5. Nancy S. Tobler, "Meta-Analysis of 143 Adolescent Drug Prevention Programs: Quantitative Outcome Results of Program Participants Compared to a Control or Comparison Group," *Journal of Drug*

Issues, vol. 16 (1986), 537–67. Tobler discusses her further analysis of the most promising ninety-one programs in "Drug Prevention Programs Can Work: Research Findings," *Journal of Addictive Diseases,* vol. 11, no. 3 (1992), 1–28.

6. Ellen R. Morehouse, personal communication, January 15, 1991.

7. Smart Moves, which is designed specifically for pre-teenage children, was evaluated by Dr. John D. Swisher of Pennsylvania State University, and reported in Gale Barrett-Kavanagh, program director, "Boys Clubs of America's National Prevention Program," Executive Summary Report, 1989. Subsequent evaluation of Stay Smart, the follow-up prevention program aimed at thirteen- to fifteen-year-olds, and Smart Leaders, a two-year booster program for older teenagers, found that participants reported less marijuana, alcohol, and cigarette use than teenagers not in the programs. See Tena L. St. Pierre, D. Lynne Kaltreider, Melvin M. Mark, and Kathryn J. Aikin, *Booster Sessions: A Targeted Demonstration Approach to Prevent Alcohol and Other Drug Use, and Early Sexual Activity* (University Park, Pa.: Center for Health Policy Research, Pennsylvania State University, November 1991).

8. Roxanne Spillet, Errol Sewell, Kristin Cole, Steven Schinke, and Mario Orlandi, "Boys and Girls Clubs in Public Housing Projects: Prevention Services for Youth at Risk," unpublished paper, 1990. Copies can be obtained from Steven Schinke, Columbia University School of Social Work, 622 West 113th Street, New York, N.Y. 10025.

9. David Hawkins and Richard Catalano, "Risk and Protective Factors for Alcohol and Other Drug Problems in Adolescence and Early Adulthood: Implications for Substance Abuse Prevention," *Psychological Bulletin* (in press). Most recent findings are based on personal communication, January 29, 1992. Beatrix A. Hamburg, "Life Skills Training: Preventive Interventions for Young Adolescents," *Report of the Life Skills Training Working Group,* Carnegie Council on Adolescent Development (Washington, D.C., April 1990), provides valuable insight into how Life Skills Training might prevent a number of adolescent behavior problems.

10. Karol L. Kumpfer, *Safe Haven African American Parenting Project: Second Year Evaluation, July 1993* (Salt Lake City: University of Utah College of Health, 1993), and unpublished evaluation reports submitted to the Office of Substance Abuse Prevention (OSAP), Washington, D.C. See also Karol Kumpfer, "Prevention of Substance Abuse: A Critical Review of Risk Factors and Prevention Strategies," in D. Shaffer and I. Phillips, eds., *Project Prevention* (Washington, D.C.: American Academy of Child and Adolescent Psychiatry, 1988); and Joseph DeMarsh and Karol Kumpfer, "Family-Oriented Interventions for the Prevention of Chemical Dependency in Children and Adolescents," in Stephanie Esekoye, Karol Kumpfer, and William Bukoski, eds., *Childhood and Chemical Abuse: Prevention and Intervention* (New York: Haworth Press, 1986). This volume is a useful reference on children at high risk for substance abuse.

11. The retention rate in Detroit is higher now that the trainers are more experienced in retaining families. The 1993 pilot test in Iowa had almost no dropout of the families who began the program.

12. For a comprehensive, insightful discussion of effective programs for children growing up in poverty, see Lisbeth B. Schorr, *Within Our Reach: Breaking the Cycle of Disadvantage* (New York: Doubleday, 1988).

5. Dealing with Dealers

1. An excellent resource is Roger Conner and Patrick Burns, *The Winnable War: A Community Guide to Eradicating Street Drug Markets* (Washington, D.C.: American Alliance for Rights and Responsibilities, 1994).

2. Mark A. R. Kleiman and Kerry D. Smith, "State and Local Drug Enforcement: In Search of a Strategy," in Michael Tonry and James Q. Wilson, eds., *Drugs and Crime* (Chicago: University of Chicago Press, 1990). See also Robert MacCoun and Peter Reuter, "Are the Wages of Sin $30 an Hour? Economic Aspects of Street-Level Drug Dealing," *Crime and Delinquency*, vol. 38, no. 4 (October 1992), 477–91.

3. *National Drug Control Strategy 1994.*

4. Peter Reuter, Robert MacCoun, and Patrick Murphy, *Money from Crime: A Study of the Economics of Drug Dealing in Washington, D.C.* (Santa Monica, Calif.: Rand Corporation, June 1990).

5. Conner and Burns, *The Winnable War.*

6. Nancy Kates, "REACH: Fighting Crack and Crime in Pilgrim Village, Detroit," case study for use at the John F. Kennedy School of Government, Harvard University, Cambridge, Mass., 1990.

7. Mark A. R. Kleiman, "Crackdowns, the Effects of Intensive Enforcement on Retail Heroin Dealing," Working Paper series no. 88-01-11, John F. Kennedy School of Government, Harvard University, 1988.

8. Alison Frankel and Lisa Freeland, "Is Street-Level Enforcement a Bust?" *The American Lawyer*, March 1990, 101–109. See also R. J. Toledo, "A Study of Drug Activity in South Jamaica Queens Area Following Special Police Efforts to Reduce Drug Dealing," internal report, New York State Department of Substance Abuse Services, 1988. I have also relied on Sally Hillsman, Susan Sadd, Mercer Sullivan, and Michele Sviridoff, "The Community Effects of Street-Level Narcotics Enforcement: A Study of the New York City Police Department's Tactical Narcotics Teams," draft report, Vera Institute of Justice, New York, May 1989.

9. Data provided by the Pasadena Police Department, February 1992.

10. A 1992 federal law requires states to adopt "use it and lose it" legislation revoking drivers' licenses for six months or more for those convicted of drug offenses. States that fail to comply will lose 10 percent of their highway funds by 1995. Although legislatures have the option to vote not to comply, it is unlikely that many will do so. These measures enjoy widespread political support, even though they raise possible compromises of constitutional protections. However, the recent U.S. Supreme Court decision upholding mandatory life sentences for first-time drug dealers suggests that challenges to the "use it and lose it" legislation as unconstitutional "cruel and unusual punishment" would not succeed. In the past decade, the courts have become increasingly restrictive in interpreting the rights of individuals convicted of drug offenses. For further discussion, see Franklin E.

Zimring and Gordon Hawkins, *The Search for Rational Drug Control* (New York: Cambridge University Press, 1992).

11. For a vivid account of street dealing, see Terry Williams, *The Cocaine Kids* (Reading, Mass.: Addison-Wesley, 1989). See also Bruce Johnson, Terry Williams, Kojo Dei, and Harry Sanabria, "Drug Abuse in the Inner City: Impact on Hard-Drug Users and the Community," in Tonry and Wilson, *Drugs and Crime*, 9–67.

6. Driving Drugs from the Workplace

1. Joseph B. Treaster, "For Transit Union, a Change of Heart on Drug Testing," *New York Times,* August 30, 1991.

2. *Household Survey 1992* (see chapter 1, note 1).

3. Testimony of Joseph H. Autry III, National Institute of Drug Abuse, at a hearing before the Committee on Small Business, Subcommittee on Regulation, Business Opportunities, and Energy, U.S. House of Representatives, March 8, 1991. See also *Research on Drugs and the Workplace*, NIDA Capsules Series no. C-87-2 (Washington, D.C., 1990). *Drugs in the Workplace: Research and Evaluation Data,* NIDA Research Monograph 91 (Rockville, Md.: Government Printing Office, 1989), provides comprehensive information on prevalence of employee drug use, its relationship to productivity, and industry responses.

4. An excellent resource on corporate employee assistance and drug testing programs is *Corporate Experiences with Drug Testing Programs,* Research Report no. 941, the Conference Board (New York, 1990). See also Thomas E. Backer, *Strategic Planning for Workplace Drug Abuse Programs,* U.S. Department of Health and Human Services (DHHS pub. no. [ADM] 87-1538, 1987) for practical guidance as well as descriptions of model programs, including Wells Fargo Bank and Union Carbide.

5. *1994 American Management Association Survey of Workplace Drug Testing and Drug Abuse Policies* (New York: American Management Association, 1994). See also J. Michael Walsh and Jeanne G. Trumble, "The Politics of Drug Testing," in Robert H. Coombs and Louis Jolyon West, eds., *Drug Testing: Issues and Options* (New York: Oxford University Press, 1991), 22–49.

6. For current developments in workplace programs and related policy issues, I have drawn on two newsletters: *The National Report on Substance Abuse*, published biweekly by Buraff Publications in Washington, D.C.; and *Drug Detection Report*, published twice a month by Pace Publications in Washington, D.C.

7. For an excellent review of the literature and a detailed analysis of the many issues raised by drug testing, see Diana C. Walsh, Lynn Elinson, and Lawrence Gostin, "Worksite Drug Testing," *Annual Review of Public Health*, vol. 13 (1992), 197–221.

8. *Gallup Survey 1989* (see chapter 1, note 3). For a thorough discussion of the role of drug testing in preventing employee drug use, see Terry C. Blum and Paul M. Roman, "Drug Prevention Strategies in the Workplace," in Robert H. Coombs and Douglas Ziedonis, eds., *Handbook of Drug Abuse Prevention* (Boston: Allyn and Bacon, 1994).

9. Robert Coombs and Frank Ryan, "Drug Testing Effectiveness in Identifying and Preventing Drug Use," *American Journal of Drug and Alcohol Abuse*, vol. 16, nos. 3 and 4 (1990), 173–84.

10. Howard V. Hayghe, "Anti-drug Programs in the Workplace: Are They Here to Stay?" *Monthly Labor Review*, vol. 114, no. 4 (April 1991), 26–29.

11. Susan A. Berger, Elena Brown Carr, and Jeffrey Mintzer, *Evaluation of the Small Business Project: Innovations, Challenges, and Future Directions* (Washington, D.C.: Corporation Against Drug Abuse, 1993).

7. TREATING ADDICTION

1. A Gallup poll conducted in January 1990 found that only 5 percent of Americans think that treatment should be the primary focus of government antidrug efforts. Kathleen Maguire and Timothy J. Flanagan, eds., *Sourcebook of Criminal Justice Statistics 1990*, U.S. Department of Justice, Bureau of Justice Statistics (Washington, D.C.: Government Printing Office, 1991), table 2.96.

2. See *National Drug Control Strategy 1994*, 77; and *The Effectiveness of Drug Abuse Treatment: Implications for Controlling AIDS/HIV Infection*, Background Paper no. 6 (Washington, D.C.: Office of Technology Assessment, U.S. Congress, September 1990), 56–57.

3. For a comprehensive review of treatment effectiveness, see the *IOM Study*, chapter 5, and Herbert D. Kleber, "Treatment of Drug Dependence: What Works," *International Review of Psychiatry*, vol. 1 (1989), 81–100. For discussion of factors related to recovery, see Joseph Westermeyer, "Nontreatment Factors Affecting Treatment Outcome in Substance Abuse," *American Journal of Drug and Alcohol Abuse*, vol. 15, no. 1 (1989), 13–29.

4. Richard A. Rawson, "Cut the Crack: The Policymaker's Guide to Cocaine Treatment," *Policy Review*, Winter 1990, 10–19.

5. See the *IOM Study*, 1990, pp. 170–74, for a discussion of chemical dependency treatment (also called the Minnesota model, twenty-eight-day, twelve-step, or Hazleden-type treatment) and a summary of the very limited evaluations of its effectiveness. More recently, a two-year study of employees referred for treatment of alcohol and cocaine abuse found that those assigned to compulsory inpatient programs did better than those who attended only AA meetings. See Diana C. Walsh, Ralph W. Hingson, Daniel M. Merrigan, et al., "A Randomized Trial of Treatment Options for Alcohol-Abusing Workers," *New England Journal of Medicine*, vol. 325 (September 12, 1991), 775–82.

6. For an overview of therapeutic community treatment, see George De Leon and Mitchell S. Rosenthal, "Treatment in Residential Therapeutic Communities," in T. B. Karasu, ed., *Treatments of Psychiatric Disorders*, vol. 2 (New York: American Psychiatric Press, 1989), 1379–96.

7. For an excellent review of treatment research since 1980, see M. Douglas Anglin and Yih-Ing Hser, "Treatment of Drug Abuse," in Michael Tonry and James Q. Wilson, eds., *Drugs and Crime* (Chicago: University of Chicago Press, 1990), 393–460.

8. See chapter 2, note 20.

9. For a concise summary of research on the effectiveness of methadone maintenance, see *Effectiveness of Drug Abuse Treatment*, 67–77.

10. Recent research confirms that all drug treatment lowers drug use and crime for at least some period of time. After that, family problems, employment skills, and psychiatric problems determine the relative effectiveness of various treatment approaches. Classifying

patients according to a "problem severity profile," a major study found that low-severity patients (approximately 15 percent, those without psychiatric problems) did extremely well in all types of treatment programs and showed the highest level of improvement. High-severity patients (20 percent, who have serious depression and anxiety) did very poorly, regardless of the type of program. The mid-severity group (65 percent of the total, with moderate symptoms of anxiety and depression) showed a range of outcomes depending on the type of program. For this group, matching types of patients with specific programs was shown to improve outcomes. See Charles P. O'Brien, *Treatment Research, Second Triennial Report on Drug Abuse and Drug Abuse Research*, DHHS pub. no. (ADM) 87-1486 (Washington, D.C.: Government Printing Office, 1987).

11. *IOM Study*, 1990. For additional analysis of the cost and benefits of drug treatment, see Robert Hubbard, Mary Ellen Marsden, J. Valley Rachal, et al., *Drug Abuse Treatment: A National Study of Effectiveness* (Chapel Hill: University of North Carolina Press, 1989), 158–61. The authors conclude that "these benefits appear to be at least as large as the cost of providing treatment, and much of the cost is captured during the treatment. Post-treatment gains are virtually an economic bonus."

12. See *Fighting Drug Abuse: New Directions for Our National Strategy*, prepared by the Majority Staffs of the Senate Judiciary Committee and the International Narcotics Control Caucus, February 1991, 9. See also *Drugs, Crime and the Justice System* (Washington, D.C.: Bureau of Justice Statistics, 1993).

8. TREATING CRIMINAL OFFENDERS

1. U.S. Department of Justice, Federal Bureau of Investigation, *Crime in the United States, 1992*, 217. See also U.S. Department of Justice, Federal Bureau of Investigation, *Crime in the United States, 1982*.

2. Linda Greenhouse, "Mandatory Life Term Is Upheld in Drug Cases," *New York Times*, June 28, 1991.

3. A February 1994 Department of Justice report concluded that "low-level" nonviolent drug law violators comprised just over one-

fifth of the total federal prison population. Most received mandatory minimum sentences, serving an average of at least five years before release. Low-level federal drug offenders are receiving much longer sentences than they were before the passage of the 1986 Anti-Drug Abuse Act, even though other research shows that a short sentence has the same deterrent effect as a long one for this type of offender. See *An Analysis of Non-Violent Drug Offenders with Minimal Criminal Histories* (Washington, D.C.: U.S. Department of Justice, February 1994). In federal prisons, the inmate population increased by more than half from 1986 to 1991, with a 139 percent jump in the proportion of inmates convicted of drug-related offenses, according to *Drug Treatment: Despite New Strategy, Few Federal Inmates Receive Treatment*, GAO/HRD-91-116 (Washington, D.C.: General Accounting Office, September 1991), 2. Nearly 60 percent of federal prisoners were serving time for drug offenses in *Drug and Crime Facts, 1992* (Washington, D.C.: Bureau of Justice Statistics, 1993), p. 18.

4. Charles S. Clark, "Prison Overcrowding," *CQ Researcher*, February 4, 1994, 99–106. See Joan Petersilia, Joyce Peterson, and Susan Turner, *Evaluating Intensive Probation and Parole Supervision Programs: Results of a Nationwide Experiment* (Santa Monica, Calif.: Rand Corporation, August 1991); and James Austin, "The Consequences of Escalating the Use of Imprisonment: The Case Study of Florida," *NCCD Focus*, June 1991.

5. See *Crime Sourcebook 1992*, 600, 610–11.

6. Sarah Lyall, "Without the Money to Supply Prison Beds, Officials Consider Reducing Demand," *New York Times*, February 17, 1992, B5. *Crime Sourcebook 1992*, 620.

7. Petersilia, Peterson, and Turner, *Evaluating Intensive Probation and Parole Supervision Programs*, 5.

8. For a comprehensive discussion of treating drug-abusing criminal offenders, see Gregory P. Falkin, Harry K. Wexler, and Douglas S. Lipton, "Drug Treatment in State Prisons," in Dean R. Gerstein and Henrick J. Harwood, eds., *Treating Drug Problems*, vol. 2 (Washington, D.C.: National Academy Press, 1992).

9. *Drug Treatment: Despite New Strategy, Few Federal Inmates Receive Treatment,* 18; and *Drug Treatment: State Prisons Face Challenges in Providing Services,* GAO/HRD-91-128 (Washington, D.C.: General Accounting Office, September 1991), 4.

10. For a detailed review of evaluations of the Stay'n Out and Cornerstone programs, see Falkin, Wexler, and Lipton, "Drug Treatment in State Prisons."

11. Thus far, the Amity program has succeeded in keeping its inmates off drugs. From February 1, 1991, to February 1, 1992, 4 percent of the inmates randomly tested at the R. J. Donovan facility were found to be using drugs. During the same period, none of the Amity participants tested positive, although they were tested more frequently than inmates in the general prison population.

12. *Intervening with Substance-Abusing Offenders: A Framework for Action: The Report of the National Task Force on Correctional Substance Abuse Strategies,* Department of Justice, National Institute of Corrections, June 1991.

13. Information provided by the Miami Coalition for a Drug-Free Community, March 1994.

14. See Jeffrey S. Tauber, *The Importance of Immediate and Intensive Intervention in a Court-Ordered Drug Rehabilitation Program: An Evaluation of the F.I.R.S.T. Diversion Project After Two Years* (Oakland, Calif.: Oakland-Piedmont-Emeryville Municipal Court, March 1993). See also Jane Gross, "Probation and Therapy Help Some Drug Users," *New York Times,* June 21, 1991.

15. Charles J. Hynes and Susan A. Powers, "Drug Treatment Alternative-to-Prison of the Kings County District Attorney: Third Annual Report of Operations, October 15, 1992, to October 15, 1993."

16. *IOM Study,* 1990, 180–83.

17. *IOM Study,* 1990, 183–84.

18. New York State Division of Parole, *Fifth Annual Shock Legislative Report,* 1993.

19. Joan Petersilia and Susan Turner, *Intensive Supervision for High-Risk Probationers* (Santa Monica, Calif.: Rand Corporation, December 1990).

20. See Carol Pogash, "Would You Please Welcome Mimi Silbert," *Image* (*San Francisco Examiner*), July 31, 1988, and Jane Gross, "Ex-Convicts Are Serving Blintzes Instead of Time," *New York Times*, December 18, 1991.

9. BUILDING COMMUNITY COALITIONS

1. See *President's Drug Advisory Council Report on National Community Coalitions to Fight Drug Abuse* (Washington, D.C.: Executive Office of the President, January 1991).

2. See "Drug Abuse Prevention Strategy, Executive Summary," the Corporation Against Drug Abuse, June 30, 1989, prepared by Strategic Planning Associates, Washington, D.C.

3. See Herbert M. Klein, "Strategies for Action: Combating Drug and Alcohol Abuse in Dade County," Florida 11th Judicial Circuit Court, 1989.

10. CHANGING PUBLIC ATTITUDES

1. For an excellent review of recent research on the effectiveness of media efforts to prevent adolescent drug use, see Robert F. Schilling and Alfred L. McAlister, "Preventing Drug Use in Adolescents Through Media Interventions," *Journal of Consulting and Clinical Psychology*, vol. 58, no. 4 (1990), 416–24.

2. Partnership for a Drug Free America, *Media Fact Sheet* (New York, January 1993). See also James E. Burke, "Breaking a Habit of Mind," *Washington Post Outlook*, November 11, 1990.

3. W. DeJong, Jay A. Winsten, B. R. Flay, and J. L. Sobel, "The Role of Mass Media in Preventing Adolescent Substance Abuse," in *Preventing Adolescent Drug Abuse: Intervention Strategies*, NIDA Research Monograph 47 (Washington, D.C.: Department of Health and Human Services [ADM] 85-159663, 1985).

4. Information on the impact of the Partnership campaign comes from *The Attitudinal Basis of Drug Use—1987; Changing Attitudes Toward Drug Use—1988;* and *The Attitudinal Basis of Drug Abuse: The Third Year—1989—Reports from the Media-Advertising Partnership for a Drug Free America,* prepared by the Gordon S. Black Corporation, Rochester, New York. Information on the Partnership campaign is available from the Partnership offices, 405 Lexington Avenue, 16th floor, New York, N.Y. 10174.

5. Kim Foltz, "Campaign for Members Only Shifts Emphasis to Clothes," *New York Times,* November 9, 1990.

6. See Jay F. Winsten, *The Case for Designated Drivers: A Primer,* The Harvard Alcohol Project (Cambridge, Mass.: Harvard School of Public Health, January 13, 1992).

7. See "Alcohol and Tobacco Advertising: Prevention Indeed Works," *Vital Speeches of the Day,* May 15, 1993, b. 59 n15, p. 454, for an analysis of media effectiveness in preventing alcohol and tobacco use, and see Steven Jonas, "Solving the Drug Problem: A Public Health Approach to the Reduction of the Use and Abuse of Both Legal and Illegal Recreational Drugs," *Hofstra Law Review,* vol. 18, no. 3 (Spring 1990), 751–93. See also Joel M. Moskowitz, "The Primary Prevention of Alcohol Problems: A Critical Review of the Research Literature," *Journal of Studies on Alcohol,* vol. 50, no. 1 (1989), 73–74, for a good summary of media campaign evaluation findings.

8. The studies, published in the *Journal of the American Medical Association* on December 11, 1991, are reported in Jane E. Brody, "Smoking Among Children Is Linked to Cartoon Camel in Advertisements," *New York Times,* December 11, 1991, D22. In 1993, 29.9 percent of the nation's high school seniors acknowledged smoking compared to 30.5 percent in 1980—a negligible difference considering the strength of antismoking social attitudes and increased prevention efforts targeted at youngsters. Daily smoking increased 10 percent among eighth and tenth graders. *Johnston Survey 1993.*

9. Kenneth E. Warner, "Selling Health: A Media Campaign Against Tobacco," guest editorial, *Journal of Public Health Policy,* Winter 1986, 434–39.

10. Ron Winslow, "California Push to Cut Smoking Seen as Success," *Wall Street Journal,* January 15, 1992. See also Michael Grossman, *Health Benefits of Increases in Alcohol and Cigarette Taxes,* Working Paper no. 3082, National Bureau of Economic Research (Cambridge, Mass., August 1989).

11. *Household Survey 1992* (see chapter 1, note 1).

12. *Gallup Survey 1989* (see chapter 1, note 3). A CNN/USA Today/ Gallup Poll conducted in March 1994 found that 11 percent of Americans believe that smoking should be illegal; 32 percent are unsympathetic toward smokers.

13. *Household Survey 1992.*

11. LEGALIZATION IS NOT THE ANSWER

1. See David Boaz, ed., *The Crisis in Drug Prohibition* (Washington, D.C.: Cato Institute, 1990), for an interesting selection of essays advocating legalization. Thoughtful, highly readable discussions of drug policy choices include Avram Goldstein and Harold Kalant, "Drug Policy: Striking the Right Balance," *Science,* vol. 249 (September 1990) 1151–21; and Peter Reuter, "Hawks Ascendant: The Punitive Trend of Drug Policy," *Daedalus,* July 1993; and Steven B. Duke and Albert C. Gross, *America's Longest War: Rethinking Our Tragic Crusade Against Drugs* (New York: G. P. Putnam's Sons, 1993).

2. See Richard J. Dennis, "The Economics of Legalizing Drugs," *Atlantic Monthly,* November 1990, 128.

3. Ibid.

4. *Johnston Survey 1993.*

5. Nancy J. Kaufman, "Smoking and Young Women: The Physician's Role in Stopping an Equal Opportunity Killer," *Journal of the American Medical Association,* February 23, 1994, 629–30. See also Jane E. Brody, "Smoking Among Children Is Linked to Cartoon Camel in Advertisements," *New York Times,* December 11, 1991, D22.

6. For excellent brief accounts of British drug policy since World War II, see Geoffrey Pearson, "Drug Policy and Problems in Britain," in Michael Tonry, ed., *Crime and Justice: A Review of Research* (Chicago: University of Chicago Press, 1991); and Griffith Edwards, "What Drives British Drug Policies?" *British Journal of Addiction,* vol. 84 (1989), 219–26. For earlier history, see Virginia Berridge, "Drugs and Social Policy: The Establishment of Drug Control in Britain, 1900–1930," *British Journal of Addiction,* vol. 79 (1984), 285–304.

7. Figures provided by British Home Office, April 1994.

8. Ethan A. Nadelmann, "Drug Prohibition in the United States: Costs, Consequences, and Alternatives," *Science,* vol. 245 (September 1, 1989), 943.

9. *Household Survey 1992.*

10. Institute for Health Policy, Brandeis University, *Substance Abuse: The Nation's Number One Health Problem* (Princeton, N.J.: Robert Wood Johnson Foundation, October 1993), 28, 60.

11. Lee N. Robins, *The Vietnam Drug User Returns* (Washington, D.C.: Government Printing Office, 1973).

12. *Crime Sourcebook 1990* (see chapter 1, note 7), table 2.87.

13. *Johnston Survey 1993* (see chapter 1, note 2).

14. For comparison of European drug problems and policies, see Peter Reuter and Mathea Falco, eds., *Comparative Perspectives: U.S. and European Drug Policies* (New York: Cambridge University Press, forthcoming). See also Hans-Jorg Albrecht and Anton van Kalmthout eds., *Drug Policies in Western Europe* (Freiburg: Max Planck Institute, 1989).

15. For an excellent discussion of Dutch drug policy, see Henk Jan Van Vliet, "The Uneasy Decriminalization: A Perspective on Dutch Drug Policy," *Hofstra Law Review,* vol. 18, no. 3 (Spring 1990), 717–50.

16. J. P. Sandwijk, P. D. Cohen, and S. Musterd, *Licit and Illicit Drug Use in Amsterdam* (Amsterdam: Instituut voor Sociale Geografie, 1991).

12. TOWARD A DRUG-FREE AMERICA

1. Bureau of Justice Statistics, *Fact Sheet: Drug Data Summary*, February 1994. A 1993 Rand report concluded that source country cocaine policies are useful only to disrupt markets temporarily, but are ineffective as an overall drug control strategy. Kevin Jack Riley, *Snow Job? The Efficacy of Source Country Cocaine Policies* (Santa Monica, Calif.: Rand Corporation, 1993). See also Mathea Falco, "Foreign Drugs, Foreign Wars," *Daedalus*, Summer 1992; see also *Drug Control: Impact of DOD's Detection and Monitoring on Cocaine Flow*, GAO/NSIAD-91-297 (Washington, D.C.: General Accounting Office, 1991).

2. *Household Survey 1992* (see chapter 1, note 1).

3. Joan Petersilia, Joyce Peterson, and Susan Turner, *Evaluating Intensive Probation and Parole Supervision Programs: Results of a Nationwide Experiment* (Santa Monica, Calif.: Rand Corporation, August 1991).

4. See also *Crime Sourcebook 1992*, 592, 608; Bureau of Justice Statistics, *Fact Sheet: Drug Data Summary*, February 1994; *Facts About Prisons and Prisoners* (Washington, D.C.: The Sentencing Project, 1994).

5. Peter Reuter, Robert MacCoun, and Patrick Murphy, *Money from Crime: A Study of the Economics of Drug Dealing in Washington, D.C.* (Santa Monica, Calif.: Rand Corporation, June 1990).

6. Institute for Health Policy, Brandeis University, *Substance Abuse: The Nation's Number One Health Problem* (Princeton, N.J.: Robert Wood Johnson Foundation, October 1993), 16.

7. Jeffrey S. Tauber, *The Importance of Immediate and Intensive Intervention in a Court-Ordered Drug Rehabilitation Program: An Evaluation of the F.I.R.S.T. Diversion Project After Two Years* (Oakland, Calif.: Oakland-Piedmont-Emeryville Municipal Court, March 1993), 24.

INDEX

reasons for (why people start), 33–43

risks of, 166

social cost of, 9, 14–15, 182–83, 200

social influence and, 35–43, 166–68

statistics, 3, 52

in the workplace. *See* workplace, drug use in

drug users:

children of, 64–70, 123–25

middle class, 21–23, 111–12

minorities, 18–21, 97

number of, 9–11, 91–92, 126, 180–81

suburban, drive-through, 72, 76–77, 82, 85

youthful, 52–53, 64–70

Dusenbury, Linda, 42, 59

Earl, Lee, 78

education, antidrug:

cartoon campaigns, 169–70

expenditures for, 6

factual, 33–34, 169–70

failure of, in 1960s, 21–22

programs that work, 12

Eisen, David, 116

employee assistance programs (EAPs), 94–95, 105, 106

enforcement. *See* law enforcement, antidrug

Engelsman, Eddy, 186

Estrada, Vicki, 39

Europe, drug laws in, 184–87

Fair, T. Willard, 72, 75, 80, 81, 162, 196, 201

families:

of drug abusers, 64–70, 123–25

prevention programs involving, 38, 167

fetal alcohol syndrome, 28

Field, Gary, 134–35

Fighting Back, 154, 156

Florida, 105, 132, 138–41, 158, 192

Foote, Edward, 153

Foote, Tad, 155

Fort Lauderdale, Fla., 82

foundations, antidrug project funding by, 154

Freud, Sigmund, 17–18

Friedman, Milton, 175

Gallup, N.M., 156–57

Gates, Brad, 169

Gates, Darryl, 25

General Motors, 102

Genesis I, 116–17

Glaser, Susan, 87

Goldstein, Stanley, 29, 132, 139–41

Goplerud, Eric, 63

government, lobbying of, by community coalitions, 158–60

government workers, drug testing of, 96–97

Great Britain, 179–80, 186

group therapy, 122–25

Gutfreund, Martin, 95, 97, 98, 103, 105–6

Hansen, William, 45

Harbor Light treatment center, Detroit, 65–68

Harrison Narcotic Act (1914), 20

Hart, Ed, 57

Harvard School of Public Health, 170–71

Hawaii, 64

Hawkins, David, 64

Hazleden, Minn., treatment center, 118

Head Start, 69–70

Heard, Maryellen, 122

helplines (800 numbers), 93, 167

Herman, Michael, 38

heroin:

demand for, 5, 8

drug effects of, 203–4

number of addicts, 11, 126, 181

prescriptions for, in Britain, 179–80

public attitudes toward, 22, 183

smokable, 181–82

testing for, 95

treatment programs, 30–31, 125–28, 179–80

high schools, drug culture in, 52–53

About the Author

MATHEA FALCO is president of Drug Strategies, a nonprofit organization that promotes more effective approaches to the nation's drug problems. Before moving to Washington, D.C., in 1993, she was director of health policy, Department of Public Health, Cornell University Medical College, in New York City. From 1977 to 1981, she was assistant secretary of state for international narcotics matters. She has also served as chief counsel of the Senate Judiciary Subcommittee on Juvenile Delinquency and as special assistant to the president of the Drug Abuse Council. A graduate of Radcliffe College and Yale Law School, she lives in Washington, D.C., with her husband, Peter Tarnoff, and their son, Benjamin.